Cleon, *Knights,* and Aristophanes' Politics

Lowell Edmunds

D1714554

UNIVERSITY
PRESS OF
AMERICA

Lanham • New York • London

Copyright © 1987 by

University Press of America,® Inc.

4720 Boston Way
Lanham, MD 20706

3 Henrietta Street
London WC2E 8LU England

Printed in the United States of America

British Cataloging in Publication Information Available

Library of Congress Cataloging-in-Publication Data

Edmunds, Lowell.
Cleon, Knights, and Aristophanes' politics.

Bibliography: p.
Includes index.
1. Aristophanes. Knights. 2. Aristophanes—
Political and social views. 3. Aristophanes—
Characters—Cleon. 4. Cleon, d. 422 B.C., in
fiction, drama, poetry, etc. 5. Politics in
literature. 6. Athens (Greece)—Politics and
government. I. Title.
PA3875.E73E36 1987   882'.01   87-25247
ISBN 0-8191-6681-2 (alk. paper)
ISBN 0-8191-6682-0 (pbk. : alk. paper)

Table of Contents

Preface

I am grateful to Phyllis Culham, Diskin Clay, Thomas Figueira, Jeffrey Henderson, Kurt Raaflaub, Ralph Rosen, and Daniel Tompkins for their comments on an earlier draft of this monograph. The first and the third in this list in fact read two drafts. I am also grateful to the anonymous referee whose expert comments were forwarded to me by University Press of America. What I thought was the ultimate became the penultimate draft thanks to thorough readings by Thomas Marier and Gregory Crane. χρεῖαι δὲ παντοῖαι φίλων ἀνδρῶν. The latter also wrote the filter program that converts the transliterated Greek of word-processing into the symbols interpreted by the printer as characters in its Greek font.

Some readers of this monograph will be curious about other details of its production. It was word-processed on an AT&T 3B2 computer, operated by UNIX System V Release 2.0.5, in the Department of Classics at The Johns Hopkins University and printed on an Imagen laser printer. The text-formatting program was troff. Since the original form of this program did not provide for automatically numbered footnotes, different macros have been developed in different places to overcome this deficiency. (A macro combines basic features of an existing program—in this case, troff—to perform a specific function.) At Hopkins, the footnote macro does not treat the superscript number in the text and the immediately preceding character as a single unit. For this reason, the superscript number sometimes annoyingly appears at the beginning of a line. Another typographical oddity needs explanation, too. The Greek font used in this monograph does not include breathing marks. The opening and closing single quotation marks of the Roman font serve as substitutes. Despite these and other, less visible difficulties, the possibility of retaining control over the typography of this monograph has been one of the gratifications of working with University Press of America. Such control as I could muster was increased in many ways by Steven Klenda (G. W. C. Whiting School of Engineering of The Johns Hopkins University, '89), an expert in troff.

Despite the electronic, infinitely malleable form in which this document was prepared, revisions and additions had to cease at a certain point and the work had to be concluded with a preface. I thus use this place for some bibliographic addenda. Sommerstein 1986 should have been cited at p. 60n6. At p. 64n26, I cited Jeffrey Henderson's edition of *Lysistrata* as forthcoming. It is now out and appears in the Bibliography as Henderson 1987. I should also like to refer to a forthcoming article of his, "The Demos and the Comic Festival," of which he has recently sent me a draft. It provides support for the position I have taken in pp. 59-65 of this monograph. Indeed, this article, a masterful reconsideration of the comic poets' goals and of their audience's expectations, situates Old Comedy more precisely in Athenian political life than any other study of which I am aware.

Parts of this monograph appeared as "The Aristophanic Cleon's 'Disturbance' of Athens" in *AJP* 108.2 (1987) 233-63.

L. E.
Baltimore
July, 1987

Introduction

Knights has received a good share of literary-critical attention. Several sensitive readings bring us closer to the poetic and dramatic qualities of the play. [1] Detailed studies of comic techniques specific to Aristophanes and/or Old Comedy are available, [2] and the formal and metrical designs have received thorough analysis. [3] One could complain only of the lack of an up-to-date text and commentary. Alan H. Sommerstein provides a new text, with a brief apparatus criticus and commentary, and, in the form of a translation with stage directions, an important new reading of the play. [4] The lack will be substantially repaired, within a few years, by the edition of *Knights* that Jeffrey Henderson will contribute to the Oxford series of Aristophanic comedies.

The old bugaboo of the literary criticism of *Knights* is this comedy's dramatic unity, which is, by most accounts, seriously endangered by the unexpected final scene, in which the Sausage-seller presents a transformed Demos. We had no reason to expect, according to the usual opinion, that either the Sausage-seller or Demos was capable of overcoming his richly satirized foibles. This concern with unity rests, as E.-R. Schwinge has shown in a fundamental article, [5] on an "esthetic of representation" which goes back to Aristotle's historical-theoretical account of the development of Attic comedy. [6] This account made unity of action the principal esthetic criterion for the literary criticism of Aristophanes. Schwinge opposes to the "esthetic of representation" an "esthetic of reception," which takes the relation between comedy and audience as the starting-point for the critical appreciation of Aristophanic comedy. [7] The relation is based on the political nature of this comedy: whatever the earlier history of the genre, Cratinus (frag. 4 Dem.=48a E=52 K-H) set the standard of political utility, and in various places Aristophanes asserts comedy's rivalry with tragedy as a teacher of the citizens. [8]

From Schwinge's position, one might move in either of two directions. One is performance; and Schwinge himself offers a reading of *Knights* that, without a detailed study of all aspects of

---

[1] Pohlenz 1952; Navarre 1956:101-63; Whitman 1964:80-103; Albini 1965; Strauss 1966:80-111; Landfester 1967.
[2] Newiger 1957; Taillardat 1965; Rau 1967; Henderson 1975:66-70.
[3] Gelzer 1960; Händel 1963; Prato 1962; Zimmermann 1984, 1985 and 1987.
[4] Sommerstein 1981.
[5] Schwinge 1975b.
[6] Schwinge uses the expression "darstellungsästhetisch," in which the first element means not "performance" but "representation," i.e. of an action that is logical according, in the Aristotelian formulation, to the probable or the necessary.
[7] See also Kraus 1985:189-90.
[8] Especially *Ach.* 655-56. See Taplin 1983.

performance, for which there is still room, analyzes the action in terms of an intended effect on the Athenian audience. Aristophanes' goal is to get rid of Cleon, and the dramatic action can only be understood from this point of view. The other direction, the one followed in this monograph, is the ideological background of Aristophanes' opposition to Cleon. The attitudes toward Cleon that Aristophanes can awaken in his audience are as much a part of the "esthetic of reception" as anything in the dramatic action. These attitudes are here, mainly for the sake of convenience, referred to as "ideology," a term discussed in section 1.

In order to describe this ideology and its tradition, it was necessary, starting from various points in the text (or script!), to go far afield and even to maintain a certain detachment. This was to be a distant, not a close, reading of the play. I attempted to establish the ideological horizons within which Aristophanes' opposition to Cleon could be located. (The question to which my study was directed was thus quite different from, while it necessarily implied, the question of Aristophanes' politics, to which I turn only in the final section.) This approach led to a new interpretation of the final scene.

1. Tradition and Ideology

Whatever the answer to the question of Aristophanes' politics, the fact remains that the comedies are intensely political. Many politicians and generals are lampooned, and some appear as comic characters. Of these, the most prominent in the plays, and, for the last decade of his life, in Athenian politics, is Cleon. In his case, Aristophanic opposition and its source seem clear. Cleon, as Aristophanes saw him, was an upstart, a vulgarian, a demagogue, and a crook, and he was also a personal enemy. [1] It seems completely unnecessary to ask why Aristophanes disliked and opposed Cleon.

If, however, "why" includes the presuppositions, the prejudgements, or, more broadly, the cast of thought on which that dislike and that opposition rest, then the Cleon-portrait does not seem so transparent. I propose to start with a single puzzling element in Aristophanes' diagnosis of Cleon's demagoguery in *Knights* and to pursue it on a plan to be indicated shortly.

This element appears for the first time in the passage in which the allegory of the household is established (40-73). We find that a slave, Paphlagon/Cleon (hereafter Cleon) has gained complete control of his master, Demos, through flattery and indulgence. Cleon is thus free to engage in activities described as follows (65-66):

περιθέων τοὺς οἰκέτας
αἰτεῖ ταράττει δωροδοκεῖ

Running from one servant to the next,
he importunes them, he disturbs them, he takes bribes.

Of the three verbs, the first and the third indicate particular, definable activities. The second or central—and it will prove to be central in a broader sense—is vaguer, and, at the same time, as an item of diction, more pervasive in the play. The verb ταράττειν, 'disturb' and its synonyms, especially κυκᾶν, are often used of Cleon in *Knights*. Some statistics will suggest the importance of 'disturbance' in this play: the simplex, *tarattein,* occurs nine times in *Knights* [2] as against a total of seven times in the other extant plays. [3] Aristophanes

---

[1] See Welsh 1978; Sommerstein 1980:2-3; Lind 1985.
[2] 66, 214, 251, 358, 431, 692, 840, 867, 902.
[3] In these other plays, the compound with cυν- occurs twice (*Nub.* 1037, *Pax* 319)

1

also uses images of disturbance. In *Knights,* Cleon is a 'pestle' and 'stirring spoon' (984 δοῖδυξ, τορύνη) and a 'mud-stirrer' (307 βορβοροτάραξι; cf. 310 ἀνατετυρβακώς). In the similarity of the Sausage-seller's trade to the activities of Cleon the Knights find grounds for encouraging the Sausage-seller. When he expresses diffidence, the Knights tell him: 'Keep doing what you're doing' (213), which means (214-15):

τάραττε καὶ χόρδευ' ὁμοῦ τὰ πράγματα

Disturb and make mincemeat of (the city's) affairs. [4]

'Disturbance' is exactly the thing that qualifies him to be the successor of Cleon.

To return to line 66 ("he importunes them, he disturbs them, he takes bribes") the question that immediately arises is what 'disturbance' has to do with the bribe-taking and peculation of which Aristophanes accuses Cleon both here and in many other places. What is this 'disturbance' that epitomizes the political style of Cleon?

The rest of this monograph pursues the answer to this question in two directions. First, in the direction of tradition, where the notion of 'disturbance' will be found to be already well established in archaic poetry. Second, in the direction of fifth-century ideology contemporary with *Knights.* Here 'disturbance' will be found to belong to one side of an ideological opposition the other side of which is formed by such principles as ἡςυχία and minding one's own business. This opposition is continuous with and indeed a development of the older tradition concerning 'disturbance', as Theognis 39-52, discussed in section 6 below, show.

Each of the two main directions of inquiry requires some preliminary discussion. An example of "tradition" is the relationship of Thucydides' account of stasis (3.82-83) to Hesiod's description of the Iron Race (*OD* 174-201). The historian's analysis discovers exactly the same pattern of behavior that Hesiod had found in the Iron Race: ethical norms are not only subverted, they are inverted, as wrong becomes right. [5] This example is useful for defining my claim

---

and with ὑπο- once (*Vesp.* 1285). *Knights* contains two compound nouns that contain the base *tarakh-* (247, 306). Furthermore, in *Peace,* Cleon is called a κύκηθρον καὶ τάρακτρον (654; both words mean something like 'stirring ladle' and are here used metaphorically) and is remembered as a 'pestle' (*Pax* 269 ἀλετρίβανος) that 'stirred up' (270 ἐκύκα) Greece.

[4] I doubt, *pace* Neil 1901 ad loc., that *taratto* was a "cook's word," though its synonym, *kukao*, was. The point is that the Sausage-seller qua sausage-seller can overcome Cleon, who is thus shown to be a sausage-seller qua politician.

[5] Edmunds 1975:73-92.

concerning the relationship between *Knights* and archaic poetry. First, the relationship between Hesiod and Thucydides is conceived diachronically but not historically. Although from the historical point of view there are many differences between the two texts, e.g., in diction and style, and some innovations in Thucydides, e.g., in the attaching of the analysis to a particular historical event, the passages possess basic similarities of structure. Second, the relationship between Hesiod and Thucydides is not conceived as a matter for the history of ideas or the history of literature. Thucydides is not reflecting on and modifying an idea that he found in Hesiod (though I see no reason to doubt that he knew the *Works and Days*), nor is his treatment of the idea (i.e. of ethical inversion) continuous with Hesiod's in any aspect that would be the proper concern of literary history. The relationship between the two should thus be called traditional. The notion of 'disturbance' in *Knights* will be found to bear this sort of relationship to archaic poetry.

"Ideology" as used in the Introduction above also requires some discussion. Forty years ago, a classical scholar could use this term casually, without definition, on the apparent assumption that everyone would know what he meant. [6] Even within the field of classics, however, the term has acquired a wide variety of senses. These can be divided into the pejorative and the non-pejorative. The pejorative rest on or ultimately derive from one form of Marxism or another. [7] In general, according to the Marxist view, the beliefs of the dominant class constitute an ideology that reflects, without their knowing it, their material interests and is thus a "false consciousness." Texts will embody, usually unconsciously on the part of the author, the ideology of the dominant class, by which it seeks to maintain its advantage in the class struggle.

In classics, the Marxist concept is applied by Diego Lanza and Mario Vegetti, *L'ideologia della città*, and, more vaguely, by Fabio Turato, *La crisi della città* e l'ideologia del selvaggio nell'Atene del V secolo a.C. [8] "Ideology" does not occur very often in G. E. M. de Ste. Croix, *The Class Struggle in the Ancient Greek World from the Archaic Age to the Arab Conquests*, for the simple reason that, as a strict Marxist, he regards all ideas as growing out of the historical process (see p. 5); therefore, whenever he talks about ideas, he is talking about ideology. [9] The position is announced in Karl Marx and Friedrich Engels, *The German Ideology*, e.g.: "In direct contrast to German philosophy, which descends from heaven to earth, here we ascend from earth to heaven. That is to say, we do not set out from what men say, imagine, conceive, nor from men as narrated, thought of, imagined, conceived, in

---

[6] Vlastos 1946:66; cf. "set of ideas" on the preceding page.
[7] See Ch. 6.3 ("Marxism and the Dominant Ideology") in Butler 1984.
[8] For the complete form of the references to the authors and works cited in this excursus, see the Bibliography.
[9] For a good critique of de Ste. Croix' use of the Marxist concept of ideology, see the review by Phillips 1984.

order to arrive at men in the flesh. We set out from real, active men, and on the basis of their real life process we demonstrate the development of the ideological reflexes and echoes of this life process." [10] Marx is disavowed by Edmond Lévy, *Athènes devant la défaite de 404: Histoire d'une crise idéologique*, but Lévy's own concept of ideology is left unclear. G. E. R. Lloyd, *Science, Folklore and Ideology: Studies in the Life Sciences in Ancient Greece* uses the Marxist phrase "dominant ideology" but without the notion of class struggle.

"Ideology" in the non-pejorative or neutral sense usually refers to a cohesive complex of ideas, beliefs, and values. This is the sense in which "ideology" is used in this monograph, and the term looks, furthermore, primarily to groups of persons, not to any individual (in which case it would be better to speak of an idea, a philosophy, a position, or the like) and to the political goals of these persons (since ideology, unlike philosophy, is typically oriented to action). [11] In this sense of the word, there can be more than one ideology at a given time, and thus a text may contain more than one, as *Knights* will be seen to do. For this reason, *Knights* is not here treated as in itself an ideological text. In my opinion, it is impossible to show that Aristophanes is governed by any ideology, either by the ones to be discussed or by any other, including "the ideology of the city." [12] Indeed, Aristophanes seems to enjoy caricaturing ideologies, and it is in this form that they appear in his comedies. [13] At the same time, as caricatures, these ideologies belong to social reality, and *Knights* can thus be read, at least to some extent, as a source for the history of Athenian social and political attitudes.

---

[10] Marx and Engels 1959:247.

[11] Cranston 1975:194-98. An example of "ideology" applied in classics in something like this sense is Loraux 1973:13-42. She describes an ideological division within Athenian recollection of the Persian Wars—oligarchic emphasis on Marathon, the hoplite battle, and democratic emphasis on Salamis, the naval battle. For an indication of the period in which this division began to develop, see Stesimbrotus, cited below in section 8. In Aristophanes, the Marathonomachae are not portrayed as oligarchic.

[12] On which see Lanza and Vegetti 1977:12-27. The interpretation of texts on the basis of ideology in a Marxist sense is, of course, obliged to proceed from Marxist premises. Therefore an author's ideology, whether or not unconscious, is determined by historical, material conditions. In a book like Lanza 1977, otherwise enlightening, the premises return like a litany: for example, "sistema ideologico come problema di produzione sociale, risultato storicamente necessario di una specifica condizione materiale" (p. 186).

[13] To this extent I agree with Lanza 1977:x that ideology is mediated in texts and cannot be taken as a direct reflection of social reality.

4

2. 'Disturbance' in Tradition

To work toward a sense of the meaning of 'disturbance' in tradition, I begin with a brief review of the semantics of *tarattein*. Its etymology has not been established, and we depend entirely upon usage. From the time of epic, a clear semantic differentiation manifests itself. Four main uses, which will persist down into Hellenistic times, are already apparent, and it is impossible to say that any of the four is derived from or is metaphoric of another. The uses are: 1. of horses; 2. of the person (either the mind or the body); 3. of bodies of water; 4. of groups of persons. The following thumbnail sketches of the four include the earliest references, in each case epic, a few illustrative examples, and the occurrences in *Knights*.

1. 'Disturbance' of horses. One of Nestor's horses, struck by an arrow, 'disturbed' (ἐτάραξε) the rest of the team and the chariot (*Il.* 8.86). The verb is, in fact, *vox propria* for the startling of horses and is so used by that master equestrian, Xenophon (*Eq.* 9.4). Taraxippus 'Disturber of Horses' was a demon that inhabited racecourses (Paus. 6.20.15-19; *Anth. Pal.* 14.4). In allusion to this demon, Cleon in *Knights* is called Taraxippostratus 'Disturber of the Horse Troops' (247). The scholiast on line 246 cites Theopompus (*FGrH* 115F93) for the Knights' (unspecified) provocation of Cleon and his attempt at retaliation. [1] The conflict between the Knights and Cleon was probably the immediate cause of Aristophanes' writing the play, as a remark in *Acharnians* (301-302) suggests. [2]

2. *Tarattein* refers to personal disturbance, mental or physical. [3] In *Batrachomyomachia,* the effect on the Frogs of Cheesecarver's declaration is: ἐτάραξε φρένας (*Batr.* 145). The φρένες (Aesch. *Ch.* 1056; Pind.*Ol.* 7.30; Eur. *Herc.* 1091), the γνώμη (Theog. 1222 W), the ψυχή (Dem. B297-98a; Gorg. B11) are places that may be affected (cf. Archil. frag. 128.1 W). *Tarattein* describes Croesus' grief at the death

---

[1] For an excellent emendation in the Theopompus fragment see Fornara 1973:24.

[2] The Aristophanic allusions to the conflict are to the Knights as a group. In reality, whereas Cleon could attack them as a group (e.g., by imposing an *eisphora* or by diminishing the *katastasis*), they would have responded not as a group but through the actions of individual Knights. See Bugh 1979:184-185, who traces the stages in the relations between Cleon and the Knights.

[3] On ταραχή in the Hippocratic corpus, see Vlastos 1946:68 and n. 36; Clay 1972:65 and n. 19. Cf. Hdt. 7.46.3; Solon frag. 13.61 W. Cf. θράccω 'trouble', 'disquiet', formed on the intransitive perfect of ταράττω, τέτρηχα.

of his son (Hdt. 1.44.1).

The verb can also refer to personal harassment. In *Knights,* the Sausage-seller, in emulation of Cleon, boasts that he will 'disturb' Nicias (358). One of the two slaves in the prologue of the play, who are persecuted by Paphlagon/Cleon, may have been the impersonation of Nicias. [4] This slave does not reappear after his exit at line 154. Whatever his identity, we know that what Cleon is said to do in the prologue of the play, Cleon did in real life—he was the enemy of Nicias (Thuc. 4.27.5)—and it is appropriate that, as the worthy successor of Cleon, the Sausage-seller should continue the harassment of Nicias. Furthermore, he turns this Cleonic form of intimidation on Cleon himself (902). In the protracted dispute between Aristophanes and Cleon, the latter 'stirred up' (verb ὑποταράττω) the poet (*Vesp.* 1285).

3. *Tarattein* refers to the stirring up of bodies of water. [5] A camel will not drink from a river until he has riled it up (verb cυνταράττειν: Arist. *HA*595^{b}30-596^{a}1). The storm in Book 5 of the *Odyssey* arose when Poseidon 'disturbed the sea' (285; same phrase at 304) with his trident. The sea remains a locus of this 'disturbance' (Aesch. Pr. 1089; Pind. *Ol.* 2.63; Eur. *Tr.* 88, 692; Dem. B14.7; Arist. *Prob.* 944^{b}22-23). The calmness of the sea, on the other hand, would become the "dominant metaphor in Epicurus' moral thought" [6] for the state of non-disturbance, *ataraxia.*

This use of *tarattein* is very productive of metaphors in *Knights.* Cleon is a wind that 'disturbs' land and sea (431), and the Sausage-seller is a boat tossed by this storm (430-41). In particular, Cleon blows cυκοφαντίαc 'dishonest prosecutions' (437). The passage can be read as a comic adaptation of the traditional ship-of-state metaphor. [7] Stormy Cleon is a recurring image. He is 'the typhoon [8]

---

[4] Contra: Dover 1959. Pro: Sommerstein 1980.
[5] Bechtel 1914:308 called attention to a group of apparent cognates in Baltic languages that have to do with bad weather. Further references in Frisk 1960 s.v. θράccω.
[6] Clay 1972:65. Cf. Plato *Symp.* 197c.
[7] Gentili 1984:322-23 provides a chart of the conventional elements of diction in nine examples of the ship-of-state metaphor. These elements are divided into fifteen categories, which appear in horizontal columns. The diction of *Knights* 430-41 and 756-57 corresponds to these categories as follows: 431~col. 2; 434~col. 5; 436~col. 6; 757~col. 9; 433~col. 13. Cf. also μέγαc (430) with Alcaeus 326.8 L-P. Cf. Komornicka 1964:53-54, who speaks of "la bataille navale, la navigation, les tempêtes sur mer" in this passage but does not speak of the ship-of-state metaphor. Taillardat 1965:180-84 discusses the passage in *Eq.* (i.e. 430-41) but sees only metaphors for anger. At the same time, he shrewdly calls attention (p. 183, n.4) to the resemblance of *Eq.* 691-92 to a line (680) in Theognis' ship-of-state metaphor, which is discussed in this monograph below.
[8] Or perhaps Typhon. So Neil 1901 ad loc. For Cleon as Typhon/Typhoeus, cf. Platnauer 1964 on *Pax* 756 and Macdowell 1971 on *Vesp.* 1033. Typhon is the archetype of hostility to order and civilization. See Griffith 1983 on *PV* 351-72.

and the whirlwind' (511). When he appears on stage, he seems to the Sausage-seller to be driving a surge before him and 'disturbing and stirring up' things (692 ταράττων καὶ κυκῶν). At the beginning of the contest before Demos, the Sausage-seller again becomes a boat buffeted by Cleon (756-7; cf. 761-2, where the metaphor changes slightly to a sea-battle). Later in the play, Cleon is beating the sea with his oar (830), but, as the Sausage-seller begins definitely to get the upper hand, the Knights felicitate him on his prospects. As the successor to Cleon, he will rule the allies with the trident (like Poseidon) [9] and will extort a great deal of money cείων, which at first seems to mean 'brandishing', i.e. the trident, but with the addition of ταράττων 'disturbing' acquires its metaphorical sense, which refers to the activity of sycophancy. [10]

Of the other examples only one will be discussed here. It is a rather fully developed simile in which Cleon's activities in politics are compared to the methods of eel-fishers (864-67):

> ὅπερ γὰρ οἱ τὰς ἐγχέλεις θηρώμενοι πέπονθας.
> ὅταν μὲν ἡ λίμνη καταστῇ, λαμβάνουσιν οὐδέν·
> ἐὰν δ' ἄνω τε καὶ κάτω τὸν βόρβορον κυκῶσιν,
> αἱροῦσι· καὶ cὺ λαμβάνεις, ἢν τὴν πόλιν ταράττῃς.

You've come to be exactly like the eel-fishers.
When the pond is calm, they get nothing,
but if they stir the mud up and down,
they make their catch. You too get something, if you disturb the city.

Cleon, then, who has already been called the 'mud-stirrer' (307 βορβοροτάραξι) uses this 'disturbing' of the city as a means of enriching himself. The connection with line 66, quoted at the beginning of this monograph ('he importunes them, he disturbs them, he takes bribes') is obvious, and makes it clear that 'disturbance' is the necessary precondition for Cleon's peculation.

4. *Tarattein* refers to the disturbance of groups of persons. In the first book of the *Iliad*, Hephaestus urges Hera to acquiesce to Zeus, that Zeus may not 'disturb the feast' (579). [11] In epic, an assembly may be 'disturbed' (*Il.* 2.95; 7.345-46). When armies and navies

---

[9] The picture of Poseidon at *Od.* 5.291-97 contributes not only to *Eq.* 839-40 but also to 431 and 692 (with which cf. also Alcaeus 326.2 L-P, quoted below in the text of this monograph).
[10] Aristoph. *Dait.* frag. 219 K; Dicaearchus *FHG* 2.255. Cf. *Pax* 653-54; the sycophant as a vessel in which to 'stir up' (ἐγκυκᾶcθαι) the affairs of the city in *Ach.* 936-40; and the connection of 'stirring' and peculation at *Lys.* 489-91.
[11] A feast should take place in 'tranquillity': Solon frag. 4.9-10 W (ἡcυχία); Hipp. frag. 26.1-3 W.

are thrown into confusion they may also be so described. In Thucydides, words formed on the *tarakh-* base occur, for example, thrice in the description of the sea battle off Naupactus (2.84.2-3), thrice in that of the night battle at Syracuse (7.44), and thrice in that of the Athenian retreat (7.80.3, 81.2, 84.4). Such words are powerfully expressive of disorder in Thucydides (note especially 4.96.3, where Athenians mistakenly kill one another). 'Disturbance' afflicts armies and navies in Herodotus and Xenophon, too. [12]

Words formed on the *tarakh-* base also refer to 'disturbance' within the polis. Citizens are 'disturbed' (Theog. 219 W). In Aeschylus' *Septem*, Amphiaraus calls Tydeus a 'disturber of the city' (572 τῆς πόλεως ταράκτορα). In fifth-century literature, the noun ταραχή is a standard way to designate civic discord. [13]

This political reference of the *tarakh-* base helps to explain Solon frag. 37.7-8 W:

οὐκ ἂν κατέςκε δῆμον, οὐδ᾽ ἐπαύςατο
πρὶν ἀνταράξας πῖαρ ἐξεῖλεν γάλα.

The main verb in the second line either takes two accusatives [14] or with πῖαρ constitutes a single verbal idea that governs γάλα. [15] In either case, it is a matter of removing cream from milk. The participle, however, has caused difficulty. ἀνταράξας has neither cream nor milk as its object, since stirring emulsifies, it does not separate cream. The object of this participle is δῆμον, understood from the preceding line. Plutarch's paraphrase of the poem to Phocus (fr. 33a W), brought into the discussion of frag. 37 W by Stinton 1976:160, with the phrase ςυγχέας παντάπαςιν καὶ ταράξας τὴν πόλιν, corroborates this interpretation, which has been put forward now and then [16] but has never gained acceptance. By 'disturbing' the demos, [17] one could get the cream out of the city, i.e. one could extort or otherwise wrongfully acquire the property of the rich. Solon has in mind the same tactics that are attributed to Cleon in the simile of the eel-fishers. Cleon makes his catch 'if he disturbs the city' (867 ἢν τὴν πόλιν ταράττῃς). For lines 9-10 of frag. 37 W, see Stinton 1976:161-162 and Loraux 1984.

From this survey of the semantics, it is obvious that the metaphorical application of the third usage, that is, of the 'disturbance' of bodies of water, is the one that has most affected the

---

[12] Navies: Hdt. 8.16.2, cf. 8.12.1; armies: Hdt. 4.129.2-3 (*bis*), 134.1; 9.50, 51.3; Xen. *Oec.* 8.4; *Anab.* 1.8.2. 'Disturbance' can affect also larger groups—Ionia (Hdt. 5.124.1) or all of Greece (Xen. *Hell.* 5.2.35; *Vect.* 5.8; Hdt. 3.138; Thuc. 5.25.1).
[13] Hdt. 3.126.2, 150.1; 6.5.1; Thuc. 3.79.3; 4.75.1; 7.86.4; 8.79.1; Thrasymachus B1 (D-K II.323.4 and 324.1).
[14] West 1974:182.
[15] Sandys 1893:48 on 12.5.
[16] A certain Bucholz, cited without reference by Allinson 1880:458; Masaracchia 1958:357.
[17] On the semantics of 'demos' see Donlan 1970:388-391.

characterization of Cleon in *Knights*. And it is in fact this metaphor, this stormy Cleon, that leads directly to the next stage of this monograph, which is the traditional background of 'disturbance' in politics. Cleon's very name, Paphlagon, reminds of παφλάζειν 'bluster', [18] a word that was used of the waves (*Il.* 13.798). It will be seen that Aristophanes' diagnosis of Cleon's demagoguery as 'disturbance' and his description of this 'disturbance' as a storm arise out of an old tradition of Greek thought about the polis. In this tradition, civil disorder is conceived in terms of meteorological phenomena—winds and storms—and especially in terms of storm-driven water. An oracle of Musaeus predicted that a 'wild rain' (ἄγριος ὄμβρος) would come upon the Athenians through the baseness of their leaders (Paus. 10.9.11). In the constitutional debate in Herodotus, the oligarch Megabuxus compares the demos to a storm-swollen river (3.81.2). [19] In the *Republic*, Socrates, or his argument, must swim through what he calls three waves if the *kallipolis,* the ideal city, is to be founded. [20] The tradition is so pervasive that further examples are unnecessary. In connection with *Knights*, however, one particular metaphor in which this tradition expressed itself, namely, the ship-of-state metaphor, deserves fuller discussion. [21]

In discussing the components of this metaphor, I shall use the terminology of I. A. Richards. [22] Richards called the subject of the metaphor the "tenor." The tenor is what the metaphor is about. He called that to which the tenor is likened the "vehicle." If a poet says the eye is a gazelle, eye is the tenor, gazelle the vehicle. Richards held that metaphor was impossible unless tenor and vehicle shared some characteristic, and he called this third component of metaphor the "ground" of the metaphor. [23] The ground of the metaphor is whatever the tenor and vehicle have in common. Eye and gazelle both have, for example, the capacity for quick movement.

In the ship-of-state metaphor, the tenor is internal discord in the polis and the vehicle is a ship tossed by a storm. The metaphor is complex. Ship corresponds to polis; storm corresponds to internal discord in the polis. The complexity can be increased by, for example, the addition of a helmsman who corresponds to the chief of state. The

---

[18] Cf. 919, where the word is used in the image of Cleon as a pot boiling over.
[19] Cf. the *hapax* ῥυάχετος 'rabble' at Aristoph. *Lys.* 170. With ὠθέει in the Herodotean context cf. *Eq.* 692 ὠθῶν (of Cleon). In *Ach.* 381 and *Eq.* 137, Cleon is compared to the Cycloborus ("a stream in Attica notorious for its volume and its roar when in spate": Sommerstein 1981:61) and to a torrent in *Vesp.* 1034.
[20] For references and discussion, see Adam 1920 on 449aff.
[21] I have not discussed the metaphor in oratory or in tragedy. For an analysis of the metaphor in Aeschylus, especially in *Sept.*, see Van Nes 1963:71-92. For Soph. *OT,* see Campbell 1986. For Soph. *Antig.*, see Nussbaum 1986:58-59, 72-74; also General index s.v. "Ship imagery."
[22] 1965:96-97.
[23] 1965:117.

ground of this metaphor is the common characteristics of polis and ship and of discord and storm. The common characteristics of discord and storm appear in the first stanza of Alcaeus 326 L-P:

ἀcυννέτημμι τὼν ἀνέμων cτάcιν,
τὸ μὲν γὰρ ἔνθεν κῦμα κυλίνδεται,
τὸ δ' ἔνθεν, ἄμμες δ' ὂν τὸ μέccον
νᾶϊ φορήμμεθα cὺν μελαίναι

I do not understand the liè of the winds;
the waves roll on this side
and on that, while we down the middle
are borne in our dark ship.

In the very first line, the phrase 'the lie *(stasis)* of the winds' establishes the ground shared by discord and storm. [24] *Stasis* is the normal word for the setting of the wind from a quarter (LSJ⁹ *s.v.* B.I.2.b) [25] and is thus a proper element in the vehicle of the metaphor, but it is also a word for civil discord (B.III.2), which is the tenor of this metaphor. If the very same word applies to both the tenor and the vehicle, then the ground of the metaphor, that which tenor and vehicle have in common, is given in this word. We can state the ground by generalizing the notion of stasis in such a way that stasis will cover both tenor and vehicle: stasis is a standing apart (deverbative noun from the middle ἵcταμαι), a going apart (cf. Lat. *sēditiō*), as perceived from a stable point. This standing or going apart is the ground of the negative component of the ship-of-state metaphor. Furthermore, if one compares the third and fourth semantic categories of *tarattein* set out above, it would seem that 'disturbance' is a given potentiality of both the sea and the city, i.e. that the ship-of-state metaphor has a given plausibility in the notion of 'disturbance'. [26]

What could be called a by-form of the tradition of the ship-of-state metaphor is attested in a two-line fragment of Solon (frag. 12 W):

ἐξ ἀνέμων δὲ θάλαccα ταράccεται· ἢν δέ τιc αὐτὴν
μὴ κινῇ, πάντων ἐcτὶ δικαιοτάτη.

The sea is disturbed by winds. If one
does not stir her up, she is the justest of all things.

---

[24] Silk 1974:123.

[25] Kassel 1973:102-104 has a good collection of passages illustrating this meaning. For the expression used by LSJ, viz., the 'setting' of the wind, see *OED* s.v. set *v.* VIII.107.a: "Of a current, wind: to take or have a certain direction or course."

[26] Thus Prometheus sees a stasis of the winds in the violence which has mixed up (verb ξυνταράccω) sky and sea: Aesch. *PV* 1085-88.

These two lines apparently form half of the sort of paratactic metaphor found in Solon frag. 9 W (cf. the simile in frag. 13.18-25 W). The sea would constitute the vehicle, while the tenor is the polis (or the demos?) if it is not disturbed by—'big men'? (cf. again frag. 9 W). The adjective 'justest' would be an example of "interaction" (Richards 1965:100), a "cross-terminological relation between the tenor and vehicle of an image" (Silk 1974:79, who develops Richards' concept), as 'justest', which properly applies to the city, the tenor, is applied to the sea, the vehicle. (Cf. Jacques Derrida's aphorism: "Metaphoricity is the logic of contamination and the contamination of logic" in Derrida 1981:149.) One cannot, however, rule out the possibility that 'justest' belongs to the "ground," i.e. to the common characteristics of vehicle and tenor, of sea and city. To Solon's way of thinking, 'justice' may have been a property of the sea as well as of the city. In the doctrine of Solon's contemporary, Anaximander, 'justice' (in the sense of 'recompense') and 'injustice' were key terms for cosmological processes (D-K B1), and Anaximander was hardly alone amongst the pre-Socratic philosophers in this world view. (For a survey, see Vlastos 1947:156-78.) With Solon frag. 12 W, cf. Aristophanes *Nub.* 1290-92, where, asked if he thinks the sea is bigger now than before, the second of Strepsiades' creditors replies, οὐ γὰρ δίκαιον πλεῖον᾽ εἶναι. Dover, in his note on this passage, remarks, apropos of Solon, "We might almost say that the sea 'behaves itself' if not set in motion by some external force." In any case, the verb *tarassetai* certainly belongs to the ground of the assumed metaphor. The thumbnail sketches showed that this verb applies to both sea and city, which thus share the negative characteristic of the capacity for 'disturbance'. Indeed, Solon frag. 12 W and its assumed context are built on this negative ground.

As for the positive component (polis/ship etc.), one of its several aspects calls for discussion here as defining the opposite of *stasis*. Alcaeus said, 'We [i.e. the poet and his faction] are borne down the middle (μέccον)'. The word used by Alcaeus for 'middle' is ambiguous in just the same way as *stasis*: it can be used literally of the path of a ship through the sea; [27] it also indicates a fundamental political concept. Certain French scholars have found in the 'middle' various aspects of the origin of the polis—centrality, publicity, equality, commonality— which they regard as the socio-political basis for the history of Greek thought. [28] Although within the evidence assembled by this school, certain distinctions should have been made, [29] and it should not have been assumed that the 'middle' always refers to a particular place or a particular procedure, [30] the political importance

---

[27] E.g. *Od.* 14.300: *per medium maris* in van Leeuwen's note ad loc.

[28] Lévêque and Vidal-Naquet 1964:21-22; Vernant 1971:185-7; cf. Vernant 1969:46; Detienne 1973:81-92. A useful corrective, stated apropos of Solon frag. 37.9-10 W, can be found in Loraux 1984:199-214 and Loraux 1986:239-55.

[29] Detienne 1973:83-84 does not recognize that 'to place something in the middle' (e.g. *Il.* 23.204 and Xen. *Anab.* 3.1.21, which he cites) is idiomatic for 'to offer something as a prize to be competed for' (as opposed to 'to offer something as common property to be distributed') and therefore looks to a procedure that cannot be homologized with distribution. τίθημί τι εἰς (τὸ) μέσον is a variant of the idiom τίθημί τι 'I offer something as a prize' (see LSJ⁹ s.v. τίθημι III), of which the passive is κεῖταί τι (see LSJ⁹ s.v. κεῖμαι IV.2).

[30] For example, Detienne 1973:85, believes that Theognis 678 refers to a

of the 'middle' can hardly be denied.

Given this ambiguity of the 'middle', its appearance in the ship-of-state metaphor in Theognis (667-82) is not surprising. The lines relevant to the present discussion are the following (675-78):

κυβερνήτην μὲν ἔπαυϲαν
ἐϲθλόν, ὅτιϲ φυλακὴν εἶχεν ἐπιϲταμένωϲ·
χρήματα δ' ἁρπάϲουϲι βίηι, κόϲμοϲ δ' ἀπόλωλεν,
δαϲμὸϲ δ' οὐκέτ' ἴϲοϲ γίνεται ἐϲ τὸ μέϲον·

They have deposed the helmsman,
the noble one, who stood guard with his understanding.
They seize possessions by force, and order has perished.
There is no longer an equitable division (made) publicly.

Whereas in Alcaeus *mesos* belonged to the vehicle of the metaphor, i.e. it referred to the ship and the sea, in Theognis it belongs to the tenor, i.e. it refers to the polis. [31] But this variation between the two poems, which have several elements of diction in common, is owing to the ambiguity of *mesos*, which, like *stasis*, can appear in either component of the metaphor and is thus especially revealing of the ground of the metaphor. Another place in which *mesos* belongs to the vehicle is an oracle received by Solon at Delphi (Plut. *Sol.* 14.6):

ἧϲο μέϲην κατὰ νῆν κυβερνητήριον ἔργον
εὐθύνων· πολλοί τοι Ἀθηναίων ἐπίκουροι.

Sit in the middle of the ship keeping straight
the helmsman's work. You know many of the Athenians
support you.

Here it is not the middle of the sea, i.e. the steady course through the sea, as in Alcaeus, but the middle of the ship itself to which the helmsman must cleave. The place in which *mesos* appears in the metaphor, one can suggest, is less important than the notion itself. 'Keeping straight' will be an important clue, as two couplets of Theognis will show.

They are 219-20 and 331-32 W:

---

distribution of booty; but, in the context of the Theognidea, this interpretation is impossible. As in the translation of this line offered below in the text of this monograph, the phrase *es to meson* must be adverbial. See Figueira 1985:149-150: the only "real" *dasmos* would be one believed to have been made by the Dorian conquerors of the Megarid, which would thus have determined the social and political order (in the view of the aristocrats).
[31] See Cerri 1969.

ἥcυχοc ὥcπερ ἐγὼ μεccὴν ὁδὸν ἔρχεο πόccιν,
μηδετέροιcι διδοὺc Κύρνε τὰ τῶν ἑτέρων.

Calm like me, set your feet upon the middle path,
Cyrnus, giving neither [group] the possessions of the other.

μηδὲν ἄγαν ἄcχαλλε ταραccομένων πολιητέων
Κύρνε, μέcην δ' ἔρχευ τὴν ὁδὸν ὥcπερ ἐγώ.

Do not be overly grieved at the citizens' state of disturbance,
Cyrnus, but take the middle path like me.

The first of these couplets can serve as a gloss on ἐc τὸ μέcον in 678.
The couplet says, in effect, that, if you take the middle path, you provide a fair distribution of property, viz., everyone keeps his own
belongings (cf. Solon frag. 39.4 W). In 678, then, ἐc τὸ μέcον must
reinforce ἴcoc and must be adverbial, e.g., "(made) fairly" (cf. 495,
543-46). [32] The second of the couplets just quoted shows how the
notion of the middle is antithetical to 'disturbance' (verb ταράccω), a
word that, in the context of the ship-of-state metaphor, can be used of
waves (Archilochus 105.1 W = 105.1 T) and is regularly used of the
sea (cf. the third of the semantic categories set out above). Furthermore, the two couplets, taken together, present an opposition between
calmness (base ἥcυχ-) and 'disturbance', an opposition alluded to
above (in the fourth semantic category) that will be discussed more
fully below apropos of ideology.

At this point, it is possible to state the ground of this
aspect, i.e. the 'middle', of the positive component of the ship-of-state
metaphor (polis/ship etc.). As in the case of the negative component
(political discord/storm), where *stasis* was the key, the notion of the
'middle' has to be generalized in such a way that we can see how it
covers both tenor (polis) and vehicle (ship etc.): the 'middle' is the
steady direction, the straight course, the right way to go (cf. Theognis
945-46).

The principle as such is stated explicitly, outside the diction of the ship-of-state
metaphor, by Theognis at 945-46:

εἶμι παρὰ cτάθμην ὀρθὴν ὁδόν, οὐδετέρωcε
κλινόμενοc· χρὴ γὰρ μ' ἄρτια πάντα νοεῖν.

I shall go by the rule along a straight path, to neither side
bending; for I must think out all my thoughts so that they are fitting.

---

[32] Cerri 1969:102-103 argues that the phrase does not refer to a real space but is
metaphorical and means "sotto il controllo di tutti."

The pentameter introduces another principle, indicated by *artia*. This key word, the implications of which are political (cf. Solon frag. 4.32 W), is cognate with and belongs to the same ethical outlook as *harmonia* in the sense in which Pindar uses it in *Pythian* 8 (discussed below in section 4).

Once the characterization of Cleon in *Knights* is set in the context of the traditional ship-of-state metaphor, it becomes clear that his 'disturbance' of Athens is a matter of stasis. The objection might be raised that such a characterization is too extreme to be funny: certainly Cleon was not guilty of anything like stasis as we know it from Thucydides' account of stasis on Corcyra. Against this objection, it should be pointed out that Thucydides himself recognized various degrees of stasis. [33] Verbal conflict could be taken as stasis—the cτάcιν γλώccης for which Jocasta chides Oedipus and Creon (Soph. *OT* 634-36). [34] Consider, for example, the phrase: οἱ πολῖται περὶ τῶν δικαίων ἀντιλέγοντές τε καὶ ἀντιδικοῦντες καὶ cτασιάςοντες (Xen. *Mem.* 4.4.8). These are the conditions created by Cleonic 'disturbance', in which a gentleman like Crito is not allowed to mind his own business but must fight lawsuits brought by accusers who hope that he will pay in order to avoid the trouble (ἔχειν πράγματα Xen. *Mem.* 2.9.1; cf. Aristoph. *Eq.* 258-65 quoted below.)

Another aspect of the positive component of the ship-of-state metaphor, namely, the ship, appears in *Knights* and shows another dimension of the thought underlying the characterization of Cleon as a fomenter of stasis. In the parabasis of the play, the Knights say of Aristophanes:

> he thought that one ought first to be an oarsman before trying one's hand at the helm; then after that be bow-officer and look out for squalls; and only then steer for oneself. [35]

In the immediate context, this image of a naval career applies to Aristophanes' development as a comic poet. Furthermore, this image fits with a discernible strategy on Aristophanes' part, which will be discussed below, to conciliate the rowers in the audience. [36] But at the same time, as Neil observed, the metaphor "suits statesmanship." [37] As in *Acharnians*, the comic poet again asserts the political claim of

---

[33] See 3.82.2, where the exquisite irony of ἡcυχαίτερα should be noted.

[34] In the context, Oedipus fears a plot against him by Creon. He describes what he believes to be the situation in language (618-21) similar to that of Thucydides in 3.82-83: 'If I wait in peace (ἡcυχάςων), his plans are accomplished and mine are lost' (620-21).

[35] Lines 541-3. The translation is that of Sommerstein 1981:61.

[36] By "rowers" I do not mean a faction or other self-conscious group but those persons who in one way or another depended upon this occupation.

[37] Neil 1901 on 542-544.

comedy. [38] Right after this metaphor comes the pnigos that concludes the parabasis proper. It continues the nautical theme (544-550). [39] The chorus bids the audience lift Aristophanes on a surge. The poet's justification of his former reticence is summed up: because 'he acted in a self-controlled fashion (cωφρονικῶc) and did not leap blindly in and produce rubbish' (545). [40] Aristophanes thus in passing associates himself with the ethical attitude of the Knights (cf. 334) but in the context of the nautical theme.

To sum up, the image of stormy Cleon in *Knights* belongs to the tradition expressed in the ship-of-state metaphor. 'Disturbance' and the comic version of the ship-of-state metaphor place Aristophanes' Cleon-portrait in that tradition. The same images used by the aristocrats Alcaeus and Theognis in vastly different political circumstances can now be used by Aristophanes before the Athenian audience. The tradition is thus not only pan-Hellenic; it has become, at least ostensibly, multivalent, applicable as well in democratic Athens as in the struggles of aristocratic factions in Mytilene or of aristocrats and their inferiors (Theognis 679 W) in Megara. To this extension of the metaphor from the archaic aristocracies of Mytilene and Megara to the comic theater of Aristophanes, one can compare the extension of terms like *isonomia* from aristocracy to democracy. [41]

The ship-of-state metaphor was, however, especially apt for Cleon, as Aristophanes saw him, for two reasons. First, one of the main traditional functions of this metaphor was to describe the conditions in which a tyrant emerges. Aristophanes can thus play on the Athenians' fear of tyranny. This fear is clearly reflected in *Wasps,* produced in 422 B.C., two years after *Knights*. Bdelykleon says that he hasn't heard the word 'tyranny' for fifty years but now it's commoner than salted fish (490-91). [42] In *Knights,* the new fear of tyranny is already evident, and Aristophanes wishes to direct that fear toward Cleon. [43] The Sausage-seller warns Demos of the band of young men

---

[38] With *Eq.* 510, cf. *Ran.* 686-687; *Ach.* 499-500; on the latter, see Edmunds, 1980:11.
[39] The 'eleven oars' in 546 have not been explained. References in Sommerstein 1981 ad loc.
[40] Translation by Sommerstein 1981:61 and 63.
[41] Though it is most unlikely that *isonomia* was either an early name for or synonymous with democracy: see Fornara 1970:171-80.
[42] Philokleon's quotation of Alcaeus implies that Cleon is like the tyrant Pittacus (1232-35; cf. Alcaeus frag. 141.3-4 L-P).
[43] In 447-49, the Sausage-seller brings this charge against Cleon: Your grandfather was one of the bodyguards of Byrsinē (punning on Myrsinē, the name of the wife of Hippias, tyrant of Athens 527-510 B.C.). In order to understand the joke, we have to remember that the Sausage-seller's strategy is to out-Cleon Cleon. Therefore the charge of tyranny is one that Cleon must have been using. In 1044, Demos asks Cleon: "How did you become Antileon [i.e. a tyrant] without my knowing it?" Cf. Appendix 1042-44. I disagree with Taylor 1981:181, who holds that *Knights* 786-87 (he does not mention 447-49, 852-54, or 1044) "give no hint of any partisan political taint."

15

that Cleon has around him (852-4), implying the typical bodyguard of the tyrant (e.g. Hdt. 1.59; cf. Thuc. 6.56.2, 57.1). [44] Second, the ship-of-state metaphor indicates, through the vehicle (to continue with I. A. Richards' terminology), the ship's cargo, the property of those whose ship is threatened. [45] Aristophanes' principal explicit charge against Cleon is that he steals the city's money.

---

[44] At 786, Demos asks the Sausage-seller if he is a descendant of the house of Harmodius, the tyrant-slayer. Sommerstein 1981 on 786 comments: "The point of the reference here may be that Cleon was connected by marriage with the family of Harmodius: Davies, *Athenian Propertied Families* 145, 320, 476-7, shows that his wife was probably a sister-in-law of the tyrannicide's kinsman, Harmodius of Aphidna, whom we know from *IG* ii²5765. Did Cleon exploit this tenuous connection to his own greater glory, and does Demos now expect that anyone else aspiring to be his benefactor will lay claim to a similar connection?" The suggestion is tempting, but Bourriot 1982:418-30 has shown, on the basis of an epigraphical and prosopographical analysis of the key datum (the name Cleon in a fourth-century inscription), that there is insufficient reason for positing this woman as the wife of Cleon.

[45] See Gentili 1984:263.

3. 'Disturbance' in Contemporary Ideology

In this section, I will locate 'disturbance' in contemporary Athenian ideology, in which, as I have said, it is the opposite of an ethical attitude that can be summed up in the word ἡcυχία.

Moments after Cleon appears on stage for the first time and is pummeled by the Knights, he calls for help—he is being beaten by conspirators. Justly beaten, say the Knights,

> for you eat up the public funds. . .and you pick off the out-going magistrates like figs, pressing them to see which of them is green or ripe or not yet ripe. Yes, and you seek out any private citizen who's a silly lamb, rich and not wicked and frightened of public affairs (τρέμων τὰ πράγματα 265), and if you discover one of them who's a simple fellow minding his own business (ἀπράγμον᾽ ὄντα 261), you bring him home from the Chersonese, take him round the waist with slanders, hook his leg, then twist back his shoulder and plant your foot on him (258-65). [1]

We have here in the image of fig (base *syk*-)-picking the theme of syco-phancy *(sykophantia)*, which is a fundamental mode of 'disturbance'. One of the victims is the outgoing magistrate, the other is the simple-minded rich man, who is 'not wicked' (μὴ πονηρός), thus the opposite of the Sausage-seller (180, 186, 336-337) and, by implication, of Cleon. The key terms, however, in the description of the rich man are those quoted in Greek above. They provide the basis for establishing the ideology opposed to 'disturbance'. The rich man is an *apragmon,* one who minds his own business; he is frightened of *pragmata,* public affairs, the realm to which the Sausage-seller is called (214, cf. 241, 360) and from which Cleon is finally driven, when he is banished to the edge of the city and to 'asses' affairs' *(pragmata* 1399), i.e. to the sel-ling of sausages adulterated with asses' meat. [2]

Although it is very difficult to say exactly who the Athenian *apragmones* were, [3] their views can still be described. The

---

[1] The translation, with slight changes, is that of Sommerstein 1981.
[2] I have been unable to obtain E. Spyropoulos, "ὄνεια πράγματα," *Hellenica* 33 (1981) 3-13.
[3] *HCT* 2:177-78.

rich man's principal quality in the passage just quoted, his minding his own business, belongs to a definable ethical position. It appears in an illustrative context in *Clouds*. In this play, in the debate between the Stronger and Weaker Arguments, the Stronger, who stands for traditional values, promises young Strepsiades that, if he follows his advice,

> you'll be spending your time in gymnasia, with a gleaming, blooming body, not in outlandish chatter on thorny subjects in the Agora like the present generation, nor in being dragged into court over some sticky, contentious, damnable little dispute; no, you will go down to the Academy, and under the sacred olive-trees, wearing a chaplet of green reed, you will start a race together with a good sensible (cώφρων) companion of your own age, fragrant with greenbrier and catkin-shedding poplar, and freedom from cares (ἀπραγμοcύνη 'minding one's own business', 'unmeddlesomeness'), delighting in the season of spring, when the plane tree whispers to the elm. [4]

Avoidance of the Agora (where the Sausage-seller was born and raised) and of the law courts (which Cleon haunted), exercise in a tranquil setting that breathes 'unmeddlesomeness'—a young man from this background will grow up to be the man rebuked by the Thucydidean Pericles, the man who thinks that he can play the gentleman in this spirit of 'unmeddlesomeness' (ἀπραγμοcύνη 2.63.2). Pericles has said that Athenians consider the one who does not participate in public affairs *not* 'unmeddlesome' (ἀπράγμων) but 'useless' (ἀχρεῖος 2.40.2), whereas in fact such persons consider themselves χρηcτοί 'useful ones'. [5]

The vice opposite to *apragmosynē* was, from the gentleman's point of view, πολυπραγμοcύνη 'meddlesomeness', 'being a busybody.' In Euripides' *Antiope,* Amphion says that anyone who is a busybody (πράccει πολλά lit. 'does many things') when he could refrain from so doing and live pleasantly as an *apragmōn* is a fool (frag. 193 N). [6] Furthermore, Amphion implicitly rejected the Periclean charge of uselessness. The ἥcυχοc 'quiet man' is best for the city (frag. 194 N; cf. frag. 187 N). [7] Amphion explicitly rejects the 'disturbance' that causes illness in the city (frag. 202 N). Not surprisingly, the 'meddlesomeness' scorned by an Amphion was another name for

[4] *Nub.* 1002-8. The translation is that of Sommerstein 1982:107, with minor changes.
[5] See Edmunds 1985:98 on the notion of usefulness.
[6] There are some indications of a class-distinction in the fragments (frags. 186 N, 200 N): it is a question of the appropriate way of life for one who is wellborn. The principal opposition in the play was, however, between a musical, theoretical way of life and an active, political one.
[7] Frag. 194 N is quoted below in section 4.

18

sycophancy, i.e. malicious prosecution: [8] In *Ploutos,* in a scene that, at one point, seems to allude to *Antiope* (with *Ploutos* 921-22 cf. *Antiope* frags. 193-94 N), a sycophant states that he benefits the city. His interlocutor, called Just Man, asks: 'To be a busybody (τὸ πολυπραγμονεῖν) is to benefit the city'? [9] The sycophant is an avatar of Cleon. He appears on the stage 'rushing' (cοβαρός) like the wind (872), just as Cleon 'blew sycophancy' (*Eq.* 437) and made one of his entrances 'pushing a wave before him' (692).

'Meddlesomeness' affected, however, not only internal political life, as in the matter of sycophancy, but also foreign policy. The two sides of the vice are summed up in a single line of Euripides' *Suppliants.* In this play, the Argive herald tells Theseus, the Athenian king: 'It is your custom to be meddlesome (πράccειν. . .πολλ' lit. 'to do many things') and your city's, too' (576). In Thucydides, the Corinthians blame Athenian restlessness before an audience of Sparta and her allies. Athenians consider ἡcυχίαν ἀπράγμονα 'unmeddlesome peace' as great a misfortune as laborious activity (1.70.8), say the Corinthians, and, in another place, an Athenian acknowledges, before Dorians, the πολυπραγμοcύνη 'meddlesomeness' of his city (6.87.3). [10] The 'unmeddlesome' gentleman, the one rebuked by Pericles, does not share this Athenian trait. He is anti-imperialist, [11] and would share the views of the Argive herald and of the speakers in Thucydides just cited.

The virtue on which this gentleman especially prided himself was sōphrosynē. In the passage from *Clouds* quoted above, *sōphrōn* is the only adjective needed to describe the companion who is proposed for Pheidippides. It invokes a whole ethos, which does not have to be discussed at length here. [12] Cleon's enemies were the cώφρονεc 'sensible men', [13] and chief among them was Nicias (Thuc. 4.27.5). The Knights exhort the Sausage-seller to prove, in defeating Cleon, that τὸ cωφρόνωc τραφῆναι 'the education of a sensible man' is now meaningless in public life (334, cf. 191-92). As the Sausage-seller

---

[8] In *Ach.* 382, Dicaeopolis, speaking as Aristophanes, describes himself as μολυνοπραγμονούμενοc 'filthy-troubled' (Sommerstein) by Cleon. Note in this context the verb διαβάλλω and the general similarity of the passage (379-82) to *Eq.* 258-65.

[9] 913; cf. 931 and Democritus frag. B80, which could, however, refer to foreign affairs.

[10] There have been many discussions. The main ones, in chronological order, are: Nestle 1927:129-40; 1938:21-23; Ehrenberg 1947:44-67; Grossmann 1950:126-37; Dienelt 1953:94-104; Kleve 1964:83-88; Connor 1971:175-94; Adkins 1976:301-27; Allison 1979:10-22; 1979:157-58; Lateiner 1982:1-12.

[11] Ehrenberg 1947:52.

[12] See *HCT* 3.480 on Thuc. 4.40.2 and the article in *CQ* NS 3 (1953) 65-68 there cited; North 1966.

[13] See Gomme's reflections on Thuc. 4.28.5 in *HCT* 3.469-70. I have adopted his translation of cώφρονεc. For a modern example of the attitude Gomme describes, see Strauss 1966:85.

warms to his project, one of his boasts is that he will 'disturb' Nicias (358). Despite their cheerful nihilism, shown in their support for the Sausage-seller, the Knights seem to think that they will be able to return to their upper-class life of refinement and leisure. All they want is to wear their hair long and to scrape themselves with the strigil after exercise (579). [14]

The quality of life prized by 'sensible men' is ἡcυχία 'tranquillity'. In Epicharmus, Hesychia dwells near Sōphrosynē (frag. 101 Kaibel). In the speech of the Corinthians cited above, this quality of 'tranquillity' is said to be un-Athenian; and Alcibiades blamed the ἀπραγμοcύνη 'unmeddlesomeness' of Nicias (6.18.7) on the ground that 'tranquillity' is not permitted a city like Athens. The Sycophant in *Ploutos* is, on this principle, a good Athenian. He hates the idea of 'tranquillity' and craves action. [15] Un- or anti-Athenian Athenians, on the other hand, like Euelpides and Peisthetairos in *Birds* look for an 'unmeddlesome' place (adj. ἀπράγμων 44) in which to found a new city. On this new city the 'bright [16] face of Hesychia' shines (1321-22). [17]

The hopes of Euelpides and Peisthetairos were already doomed at the time of *Birds*. Although the state of non-disturbance, ἀταραξία, would become the Epicurean ideal and in this negative form the concept of 'disturbance' would enter the history of moral philosophy, it did not have a future in political philosophy, even if it was the main concept in Aristophanes' diagnosis of the problems of Athenian democracy under Cleon and even if it was squarely situated in fifth-century ideology as one side of a fundamental antithesis, that between 'disturbance' on the one hand and calmness and minding one's own business on the other. One could say that after the time of Aristophanes this antithesis, which seems to have been a reponse to Athenian imperialism and the Peloponnesian War, lost its analytic or descriptive force. While the issue of the internal harmony of the polis did not go away, but remained a dominant concern of Greek political thought, this harmony and its opposite were conceived in other terms, which began to appear long before the end of Aristophanes' career. [18]

---

[14] The slogan they use in this passage has been explained by Boegehold 1982:147-56.

[15] On the nature of the sycophant, Konstan and Dillon 1981:376-78.

[16] Adj. εὐήμεροc from ἡμέρα 'day', i.e. a basically meteorological notion, with which contrast the darkness of the storm that threatens the ship-of-state. See the table in Gentili 1984.

[17] Eur. *Antiope* cf. frag 193 N with frag. 194 N: hēsychos is a synonym for apragmōn. Aristoph. *Ploutos* 913ff. shows the opposition between polypragmosynē and hēsychia. Antiphon *Tetr.* 2.2.1: apragmones and hēsychioi are synonyms. See especially Isocrates *Antid.* 151.

[18] Roughly speaking, the antithesis between 'disturbance' and calmness or tranquillity (ἡcυχία) was replaced by the antithesis between stasis and ὁμόνοια (e.g. Isoc. 18.44 (402/1 B.C.)). It is significant that in the earliest epigraphic attestation of a word formed on the ὁμονο- base, this word is modified by the adverb ἡcυχα (*IG*

20

4. Hēsychia in Pindar *Pythian* 8

It happens that fifth-century literature provides us with another city, Aegina, in which Hēsychia was quite at home. Pindar addresses *Pythian* 8 to this deity. A reading of this ode will supplement the many studies, cited above, of *polypragmosynē* and the ideology opposed to it. Studied as a dedication to Hēsychia, the ode provides an understanding of the truth that the Athenian *apragmones* might have claimed for their views. The ideology that, in Athenian sources, appears mainly as reactionary, in opposition to the prevailing tendencies, appears in a positive and fuller form in *Pythian* 8.

Pindar begins by asking a personified Hēsychia to accept for Aristomenes the celebration of a Pythian victory. [1] His gesture means that he will have to represent the victory of Aristomenes in such a way as to make it acceptable to Hēsychia. Furthermore, the celebration includes Pindar's ode, and for this reason the ode itself will have to be acceptable to her. Why has Pindar asked her to receive the celebration? He explains his request:

> τυ γὰρ τὸ μαλθακὸν ἔρξαι τε καὶ παθεῖν ὁμῶς
> ἐπίστασαι καιρῷ cὺν ἀτρεκεῖ.

For you know how to give and receive gentleness with unerring sense of discernment. (6-7)

'Gentleness' is a code-word for the victory-ode itself. [2] Later in this ode, Pindar will use it of his own performance (31). Hēsychia knows how to give and receive gentleness: she thus stands for both sides of the victory celebration, that of the victor, on the one hand, and, on the other, that of his family, the poet, and the others who mount the festivities. She stands also for discernment in these doings. The word καιρός indicates "the right mark or limit between the too much and the too little." [3] What Hēsychia knows how to do (verb ἐπίσταμαι) is very like that which, according to Solon, the leaders of the people do

---

[1] See Lefkowitz 1977:219-21 for a literal translation of the ode with indication of strophic division and with an outline of the conventional elements of the victory ode.

[2] Cf. *Pyth.* 1.98, 5.99-100 (depending on the reading), *Ol.* 2.90, *Nem.* 9.48, *Isth.* 2.8, and see Dickie 1984:94.

[3] Burton 1962:46. Cf. Critias frag. *7 W: μηδὲν ἄγαν· καιρῷ πάντα πρόcεcτι καλά (a saying that Critias attributes to Chilon).

not know how to do:

> οὐ γὰρ ἐπίσταντται κατέχειν κόρον οὐδὲ παρούςας
> εὐφροςύνας κοςμεῖν δαιτὸς ἐν ἡςυχίῃ.

They do not know how to restrain their insolence nor, when good times come, to order them in the tranquillity of the feast. (frag. 4.9-10 W)

A feast requires the same decorum as the victory celebration. The two occasions are governed by the same rules. [4] The leaders of the people ought to restrain their insolence (κόρος); Pindar must take care not to provoke insolence (κόρος) through overdoing his contribution to the celebration (31-32). The leaders of the people should enjoy their prosperity in tranquillity (hēsychia); Pindar dedicates Aristomenes' celebration to Hēsychia. She has that unerring sense of *kairos,* of the mark between the too much and the too little. Throughout the ode addressed to Hēsychia, Pindar will try to honor her sense of *kairos.*

Hēsychia receives the ode, then, in the first place because she is the appropriate deity of the victory celebration. At the same time, she is also other things. Pindar gives her the epithet φιλόφρων. This is the word with which the ode begins. It is a compound formed of *phron-*, indicating a mental-emotional disposition of the φρένες, and *phil-* indicating friendly. Friendly to whom? Friendly in what way? Emile Benveniste issued a useful warning on the semantics of φίλος. [5] In the places in which it has usually been translated 'friendly' or the like, the word has to do not with an affective, psychological state but with a social, to some degree formalized, relation. The Embassy in *Iliad* 9 provides a good example of friendship in this sense. [6] The *philoi* of Achilles attempt to reintegrate him into the warrior band. Odysseus reminds him that his father had counselled him to use φιλοφροςύνη in his dealings with his fellows. The Trojans know that Achilles' return to combat would mean that he had resumed φιλότης (*Il.* 16.282). The word *philos* and the various *phil-* compounds look to an institution of Homeric society, to the bonds uniting the warriors, which are not simply emotional but create a formalized 'friendship' that entails certain duties and expectations. When Pindar addresses Hēsychia as *philophron,* he has in mind her power to create such bonds. [7]

But they are obviously not the bonds of a warrior society. Hēsychia is also addressed as 'daughter of Dikā', Attic-Ionic Dikē,

---

[4] On hēsychia at the symposium, see Dickie 1984:87.
[5] Benveniste 1969:352-53, based on discussion pp. 338-53.
[6] See the analysis by G. Nagy 1979:103-109.
[7] At the level of the actual victory celebrations, the κῶμος 'victory revel' (20) was an affirmation of the ties binding the victor and his *philoi.* See Nagy 1979:241.

'Justice,' and as this daughter she bears the epithet μεγιστόπολι 'of greatest city' (1-2). [8] The epithet is echoed in the same metrical position at the beginning of the second strophe, with δικαιόπολις 'of just city' (22), which is applied to the island of Aegina. It is an island on which a just city can flourish. At the very end of the ode, Pindar prays to Aegina, here the eponymous ancestress of the island, to keep the city (πόλις) free (98-100). The bonds to which Hēsychia is disposed are, then, those that hold the city together. Hēsychia with a small h or *eta* is a political virtue. The complex hēsychia-friendship-polis is presented in the form of an argument by Amphion in Euripides' *Antiope* frag. 194 N. He states ὁ δ᾽ ἥϲυχος φίλοιϲι τ᾽ ἀϲφαλὴς φίλος/ πόλει τ᾽ ἄριϲτος 'the quiet man is a sure friend to his friends and best for the city'. [9]

Hēsychia has still further characteristics in the first strophe. She is described as 'holding the master keys of war councils' (3-4). [10] Keys are often metaphorical for restraint in Greek poetry and keyholders keep things shut in. [11] Not surprisingly, Hēsychia, Tranquillity, who, as we shall see, is close kin to Peace, restrains war councils. In the first antistrophe, however, Pindar turns to another aspect of Hēsychia's protectiveness. As well as perfectly gentle (6-7; cf. *Nem.* 4.95-96), she is also harsh (10 τραχεῖα). The enemies whom she meets with harshness are, I would argue, internal ones. [12] The bilgewater in which she sinks their hybris reminds one of the ship-of-state metaphor, which applies to the internal affairs of the city. [13] Porphyrion is Pindar's example (12). We know little enough about him, but I believe that he is here a figure of stasis, i.e. of internal discord. [14] In myth one of the two leaders of the Giants, he is 'king of the Giants' (17) in this poem. The proverb, general though it is, that Pindar applies to Porphyrion's crime might refer to his attempted rape of Hera—'the gain I like best comes from the house of a willing giver'. [15] In any case, the adjective φίλτατον and the phrase ἐκ δόμων (14) suggest that Pindar views Porphyrion not as a foreign enemy, like Typhon in the

---

[8] Edmunds 1980:1.

[9] Plut. *Mor.* 806F reports an anecdote concerning Cleon's renunciation of his *philoi* at the time of his entry into politics. See Connor 1971:91-98; Kraus 1985:170-71.

[10] Taking the phrase in line 3 as a hendiadys.

[11] LSJ s.v. κλείς I.4. Cf. Fennell 1893 ad loc.: "holding the master keys of choice between counsels and wars."

[12] So the comparison of *P.* 8.9-10 with frag. 109.3 S-M suggests: see the discussion of this fragment in the next section of this monograph.

[13] For bilgewater, see Gentili 1984:322, col. 5. The scholiast on line 14 was reminded of *Od.* 15.479, where the woman who kidnapped Eumaeus falls into the bilgewater like a tern, having been struck dead by Artemis.

[14] In Xenophanes frag. 1.21-32 W, the battles of the Giants and stasis are two of the subjects that are inappropriate at the symposium.

[15] Apollod. 1.6.2: he was killed by Heracles (cf. Hes. *Theog.* 954), though here in Pindar by Apollo (17-18). The scholiast on line 17 says that he tried to steal the cattle of Heracles.

23

epode (16), but a domestic one. [16] In the antistrophe (8-14), then, Hēsychia ensures tranquillity within the city. This is her character in other places in Pindar. [17] She is, in a word, φιλόπολις (*Ol.* 4.20). Not a passive tranquillity, she protects the city especially against internal enemies. As *philophrōn*, she actively holds the city together. Under these conditions, the city can attain greatness. *Philophrōn*, the first word in the first line of the ode, indicates the basis of the city's greatness. But so strong is Hēsychia's disposition to maintain the friendly bonds of the city that Pindar must sing at considerable length of what she would do to anyone who attempted, from within or without, to destroy these bonds. The notion of *hēsychia* does not exclude activity. For example, Xenophon says that when an army marches in good order, even if it numbers in the tens of thousands, they all move forward like one man καθ' ἡςυχίαν (*Oec.* 8.7; cf. Aristoph. *Lys.* 1224; *Vesp.* 1517). [18]

The first triad, which characterizes Hēsychia, at the end returns to Aristomenes (19-20). Apollo received him at Cirrha, i.e. Delphi, the site of the Pythian games, 'crowned with the grass of Parnassus and with a Dorian revel', i.e. escorted by Dorians. [19] —That was the first celebration, at Delphi, soon after the victory. The celebration to which Pindar's ode is a contribution takes place later on Aegina.— 'Dorian revel' is the phrase that concludes the first triad, and points ahead to the next triad, in which the victory of Aristomenes is placed in the context of Dorian Aegina's long history of triumphs in battle and in athletic competition. Elsewhere in Pindar, Aegina is a 'Dorian island' (*Nem.* 3.3), founded by a 'Dorian host' (*Isth.* 9.3). The descendants of Aeacus are a 'Dorian people' (*Ol.* 8.30), and the second triad begins with a reminder of the excellence of the Aeacids (22-24), the founding family. This second triad closes with an introduction to the myth that takes up the third triad. Exalting the

---

[16] Scholars have taken the antistrophe as referring to international relations: principally Wilamowitz 1922:443; Wade-Gery 1932:214-15, referring to the Gigantomachy pediment thrown down by the Persians; Burton 1962:176. For Cleon as Typhon, see the references in the discussion of stormy Cleon in section 2 above, n. 8.

[17] See the survey by Burton 1962:175-76, who says, "It seems. . .on the face of it that at the beginning of *Pythian* 8 Pindar is addressing the kindly spirit of civil concord." He goes on to suggest (cf. preceding note) that there may also be reference to the threat of Athens.

[18] The army in good order is in contrast to the one in disorder, which in the same context (*Oec.* 8.4) is called ταραχωδέςτερον.

[19] So Fennell 1893 ad loc. Carne-Ross 1985:173 calls attention to the contrast between the picture of Aristomenes' victory and the picture of the defeat of Porphyrion and Typhon. "If the connection between that defeat and this victory still seems somewhat remote, we may compare a passage in Olympian 13 where the victor's athletic success is seen to be grounded in the fact that his city honors Hesukhia's Hesiodic kin, Eunomia, Dika, and Eirene, and opposes brash-tongued Hubris." I shall try to show that Aristomenes' victory is grounded in exactly the same way in *P.* 8.

clan of the Meidylids, Aristomenes has deserved to have said of him what the seer Amphiaraus once said in an *ainos*. [20] Amphiaraus, who had perished in the campaign of the Seven Against Thebes, watched from the underworld as the Epigonoi, the sons of the Seven, succeeded where their fathers had failed. The seer begins: 'By nature stands forth the noble spirit that is transmitted from fathers to sons.' [21] Aristomenes' victory is, then, a confirmation of this principle of heredity.

As an, to us, amazing confirmation of this principle, Pindar concludes the myth and the third triad by stating that, when he [22] —or the chorus [23] —was on the way to Delphi, he—or they— received a prophecy from Alcmaeon, who had a shrine near his—or their— house. [24] Alcmaeon, though not known as a seer himself, was the son of Amphiaraus and the descendant of another famous seer, Melampus. Pindar says that Alcmaeon 'applied himself to the inherited arts of prophecy' (60). Pindar does not say what the prophecy was. In any case, it was another confirmation of the principle, which had already been given signal proof by the exploit of the Epigonoi.

Although Pindar does not make the connection explicit, it must be that Aristomenes as thus represented is pleasing to Hēsychia. She must like it that Aristomenes has shown himself a worthy continuator of the bloodline of the Meidylids and of the broader Aeacid inheritance. In order to find the implicit connection one must remember Hēsychia's own family. Pindar has called her the daughter of Dikē (1-2). Dikē is the sister of the Hours, Eunomia, and 'flourishing Peace' (Hes. *Theog.* 901-902). The last of these is so called because she causes cities to flourish, [25] as they can do in peacetime. In passing, I point out that the relationship of Hēsychia to Peace makes clear the connection between restraining war and greatness of the city (2-3). Hēsychia, 'of great city', is much like her aunt Peace in this respect. Eunomia, however, is of particular interest for the interpretation of *Pythian* 8. Pindar does not mention her in this ode, but, as the well known sister of Dikē, she is present at least in thought. Pindar had elsewhere called Aegina εὔνομον πόλιν (*Isth.* 5.22). Furthermore, Bacchylides had associated Eunomia with Aegina: Εὐνομία. . .cαόφρων,/ ἅ. . ./ἄcτεα. . .εὐcεβέων/ἀνδρῶν ἐν εἰρήνα φυλάττει 'prudent Eunomia who keeps the citadel of pious men in peace' (13.186-89). Although Eunomia could be used of various political systems, it

---

[20] Verb αἰνίξατο, 'uttered as a dark saying, in a riddle' (Gildersleeve 1899 ad loc.) but the statement is quite plain, as the scholiast observes. Cf. the ship-of-state metaphor in Theognis, which, plain as it is, he presents as a riddle (681). The verb indicates not the content or form of the message but the relation between the sender and the intended recipients. The conceit of such communication is that only certain persons are qualified to understand. See Edmunds 1985a:§§ 13-15.

[21] Gildersleeve 1899 on 44.

[22] For Pindar as the speaker, see Lefkowitz 1977:213 and 1975:179-83.

[23] Slater 1979:69-70.

[24] On this phenomenon, see Rusten 1983:289-97.

[25] West 1966 on 902.

was especially the catchword of the aristocratic Dorian city. [26] M. L. West has made the crucial point about the significance of the word: "It implies not so much having good laws, as a condition in which the laws are obeyed." [27]

To formulate the relation of Aristomenes' victory to Hēsychia, it is Hēsychia the niece of Eunomia who will find Aristomenes' victory pleasing. A proof of the aristocratic bloodline, the victory was at the same time a confirmation of Aegina's traditional Doric Eunomia. The persistence of the family means the persistence of the larger order and its values. (The unstated premiss is that only through the family will this persistence be guaranteed.) Eunomia is the particular form of community that Hēsychia with her kindly disposition holds together. The English adjective 'kindly', related to 'kin', is a better word than 'friendly' to translate *philophrōn*.

In the fourth and fifth triads, Pindar views the victory of Aristomenes under another aspect, the uncertainty of human prosperity, which the gods give and take away according to some indiscernible principle (76-77, 93-94). Pindar begins the fourth triad with a prayer to Apollo. The prayer is divided into two petitions, one for Pindar himself and one for the father of Aristomenes. For himself, Pindar prays that Apollo look upon every step that he now takes as poet [28] according to a certain mode (68-69). [29] 'Mode' is a translation of *harmonia,* a technical term in music, which Pindar here uses metaphorically. A mode is literally the articulation of a set of tones, the joining of these tones into a musically viable sequence. Metaphorically, then, this mode for which Pindar prays is a proper and pleasing joining of the parts of Pindar's poem and of this poem to its recipients. [30] Pindar asks Apollo to watch over his poem and to ensure that it does not fail to attain this proper 'mode'.

Mode or *harmonia* is analogous to the quality of Hēsychia indicated by the epithet *philophrōn,* the quality of maintaining the bonds of society. [31] Pindar's concern in his petition is the various bonds of poetry. The link between the two kinds of bonds, poetic and social or political, is seen in Empedocles' use of *harmonia* as a synonym of Philotēs (frag. B27 D-K), which is one of the two opposing principles in his system, the other being Neikos 'Strife'. [32] Through Philotēs all things come together (frag. B26.5 D-K). One can also

---

[26] Bowra 1961:414; West:1966 on 902.
[27] *ibid.*
[28] Burton 1962:184 and 186 on the reference of line 69 to this very poem.
[29] Burton 1962:185-186 on the phrase τιν' ἁρμονίαν and on the syntax. I take Apollo as subject of the infinitive. Cf. Wilamowitz 1922:442.
[30] Cf. Burton 1962:184-85 on the semantics of *harmonia.*
[31] On the connection of Hēsychia with music and song, see Dickie 1984:97.
[32] Cf. Nagy 1979:298-99.

compare with Pindar's harmonia the outlook, albeit rendered comically, of the Stronger Speech in Aristophanes' *Clouds*. Describing the virtues of the old-time education, he emphasizes the training in traditional musical *harmonia* (968). It was this respect for the Muses (cf. 972) that produced the Marathon Fighters. To his up-to-date opponent, the Weaker Speech, however, the Stronger Speech must appear as ἀνάρμοστος 'out of tune' (908). The poetic *harmonia* of Pindar has the same complexity, combining musical and social functions. [33]

The *harmonia* desired by Pindar in *Pythian* 8 is also related to the character of Hēsychia as one who knows how to give and receive with unerring discernment. In the lines of Solon cited above, it was clear that a traditional scene of hēsychia, where one must display the discernment attributed by Pindar to his deified Hēsychia, is the banquet. Now a proper banquet can also be described by the adjective ἁρμόδιος, formed on the same base as *harmonia*. Pindar so describes a banquet in *N.* 1.21-22. [34]

Pindar is praying, then, that his poem will have qualities that are virtually the same as those of the Hēsychia to whom he dedicated Aristomenes' victory celebration. Hēsychia's mother, Dikē, appears at the very beginning of the second petition (71). She, Pindar is sure, [35] attends the revel (cf. 22 δικαιόπολις). But Pindar must beg (72 αἰτέω) —and this is the second petition—an unenvious regard on the part of the gods for the fortunes of Xenarkes and his son Aristomenes (71-72). The latter has won often and in many places (63-66, 77-87). The rest of the poem, as Burton has observed, is dominated by the "presumption of uncertainty" in human affairs, [36] which requires Pindar's warning to his patrons. Pindar tells them that success is in the hands of god and happiness is brief. In the fourth triad, further reason for the dedication of the poem to Hēsychia is clear. She stands for *kairos,* and, given Pindar's theology, *kairos* is the best guide. [37]

In the final triad of the poem, the theme of uncertainty culminates in famous lines. These are the first three lines of the epode, which are often taken as Pindar's summa. They are balanced by a three-line prayer to Aegina that concludes the poem. The first three lines are: 'We are creatures of a day. What is someone? What is no

---

[33] Cf. ἄρθμιος, from the same root as *harmonia,* as a synonymn of *philos:* Theognis 1312 and context; Aesch. *PV* 191 and context. Cf. Schein 1985.

[34] Note that this banquet is κεκόσμηται and cf. again the lines of Solon quoted in the text above.

[35] So I take the asyndeton to indicate. Cf. Gildersleeve 1899 and Farnell 1932 on 70.

[36] Burton 1962:187.

[37] See Burton 1962 on line 77 and Radt 1958 on the closely related *Paean* 2.32-34.

one? [38] Man is a dream (made) of shadow. But when godgiven radiance [39] comes, a bright light rests upon men, and a honey-sweet life'. The dark and the bright of the final triad are thus summed up. On the one hand, the nullity of man, his shadowy existence, or worse, existence as the shadow of a dream. [40] On the other, the godgiven gleam, like the one that has shone on Aristomenes and his family. The subsequent prayer to Aegina follows without any connective: 'Dear mother Aegina, continue to conduct [41] this city in the course of freedom, with Zeus, mighty Aeacus, Peleus, goodly Telamon, and Achilles'. The asyndeton indicates an explanation of the thought of the god-given radiance. Pindar has seen this radiance in the victory of Aristomenes. It is an example of Aegina's care for her city, which he asks her to continue, with Zeus, Aeacus, Peleus, Telamon, and Achilles. These are the great names of the first four generations of the founding family. The union of Zeus and Aegina produced Aeacus, who was the father of Peleus and Telamon [42]

For Pindar's Aeginetan patrons, hēsychia contains the two main sources of political order. One lies in the quality indicated by *philophrōn,* the first word of the poem. It looks to a political community held together by bonds that are in principle family bonds—family in a very extended sense. Aristomenes' family is the Meidylids, but Pindar introduces the praise of Aristomenes at the beginning of the second triad with a reference to the Aeacids and he concludes the poem with the names of the great Aeacid ancestors. Aegina, as Pindar presents her, is an island inhabited by Aeacids. All Aeginetans are descendants of the Aeacids and thus share in the aretai of the Aeacids (22-24). Since Aeginetans have this ancestry, Pindar can say that Aegina 'has a perfect glory from the beginning' (24-25): perfect in the sense of complete, finished. [43] Any excellence or virtue that any Aeginetan may display was already there. Only that which is original can originate this virtue.

The source of virtue is thus heredity but not biological heredity in our sense. Rather, it is a *repetition* of something laid up in the origins of the Aeginetans.

---

[38] Following the interpretation of Giannini 1982:69-76, which goes back to that of L. Dissen ("quid est magnus? quid est parvus?").

[39] On αἴγλα see Segal 1976:71-81.

[40] Nagy 1986:100-101 interprets this last phrase (ϲκίαϲ ὄναρ) as 'dream of a shade', connecting it with Amphiaraus' words from the underworld (38-57). Aristomenes' victory is thus the realization of the 'dream' of the dead ancestor. This interpretation adds weight to the connection between the two halves of the epode for which I am arguing.

[41] I translate thus to bring out the force of the present imperative.

[42] Plut. *Thes.* 10.3; Paus. 2.29.2; Apollod. 3.12.6, with an alternate genealogy for Telamon.

[43] See Carne-Ross 1985:176.

According to the biology that can be assumed for Pindar, the woman did not contribute seed in reproduction, or, in our terms, did not contribute chromosomes or genetic material. Beginning in the fifth century B.C., certain doctors and philosophers began to challenge this biology [44] and to suggest that the woman had some role in determining the nature of the offspring. When, however, Pindar says that Aristomenes did not shame his maternal uncles (35-37), he is hardly thinking of qualities in Aristomenes that were inherited from his mother's side of the family. I believe that the concept was unknown to him. The maternal uncles can be mentioned only because Pindar is *not* thinking of biological heredity but of the traditions of the family. Pindar seems to me to have had a qualified view of the inheritance of virtue. He represented some individual victories as manifestations of innate virtue. At the same time, he knew many aristocrats who had never won prizes. In the very ode under discussion, "That the father of the victor almost certainly had failed or at any rate had no successes—a fact tactfully not mentioned—, seems. . .certain, in that Pindar enumerates the successes of even more distant relatives in the catalogue of the family's triumphs (35ff.)." [45]

According to Pindaric heredity, nature from time to time reveals the virtue that belongs to a family or community as an original and potentially originary characteristic that is always, as it were, lurking there. Thus Pindar has Amphiaraus say: 'By nature stands forth the noble spirit that is transmitted from fathers to sons'. The word here translated 'stands forth' (ἐπιπρέπει) really means 'to become conspicuously visible' (Hom. *Od.* 1.411, 4.64, 24.252; Theoc. 25.40), i.e. to be revealed.

One source of virtue is, then, ultimately nature as a revealing force working in and through a particular form of political community.

Generally speaking, the Dorian political community, which *Pythian* 8 links with hēsychia, is founded not on a state apparatus but on the bonds of *phylē* and of *genos*, whereas Athens, which is inimical to hēsychia (cf. Thuc. 1.70.8-9, paraphrased below), is based on institutions and laws that intend to weaken the force of the *phylē* and *genos*. Within the Ionian cities, however, a similar opposition developed. In the terms used by Enrico Montanari [46] this was an opposition between the "politico-democratic" values of Athens and the "ethnic-genetic" ones of the dodecapolis. One can add that within Athens itself there persisted the notion of the city as constituting a single genos. Athenians believed that they were descended from Apollo, [47] with the result that Socrates could say (Plato *Apol.* 30a) that he would continue his way of life examining both foreigners and citizens but especially the latter, 'since they are closer to me by race (γένει)'. In other words, all Athenians constitute a *genos*, descended, as the passage in *Euthydemus* shows, from Apollo.

---

[44] Lloyd 1983:86-94.
[45] Slater 1976:68.
[46] Montanari 1981.
[47] Plato *Euthyd.* 302c-d, on which see Hignett, 1952:57, 63; Montanari 1981:201-206.

29

The other source lies in restraint and discernment. As Hesychia is gentle and restrained but also, when the circumstances require, harsh toward her enemies, so virtue can emerge out of the apparently passive quality of restraint. Indeed, for Pindar, it can emerge only from this source, and therefore much of *Pythian* 8 is devoted to restraining the ambitions of the young Aristomenes.

The basis of Pindar's advice to Aristomenes and to his father is the theology of uncertainty. Since human prosperity is in the hands of the gods and is therefore uncertain, the safest course is an unprovocative restraint. In this way, mortals can be ready to receive the god-given gleam when it comes. The second source of virtue is, then, ultimately the gods.

To sum up, the two sources are nature and the gods. These two are juxtaposed in the final epode of the poem. As I have said, the three-line prayer to Aegina with its evocation of the Aeacid ancestors can be regarded as an expatiation of the three-line theology of the god-given gleam. The thought moves thus: when the gleam comes, life is sweet (as now in the case of Aristomenes' victory); I pray that Aegina continue to conduct the city in a way that will exemplify the greatness of her past. From the juxtaposition of the theology and the prayer to Aegina, it would seem that the functions of the gods (the first three lines) and of nature (as represented by the Aeacid founders in the second three lines) are parallel. Nature, as Pindar has presented it in this poem, makes conspicuously visible, reveals. As for the gods, when the godgiven gleam comes, a bright light is upon men, illuminates them (with 97 ἔπεϲτιν cf. 44 ἐπιπρέπει). Nature and the gods do the same things, one from within Aegina, the other from without or from above.

5. Pindaric Hēsychia and Athenian *Apragmones*

Such is the doctrine of hēsychia that can be assumed for the Athenian *apragmones*. What these persons had to face in Athens, however, was a political order founded on principles different from and even opposed to hēsychia. As the Corinthians say at the allies' conference in Sparta, the Athenians neither possess hēsychia nor allow others to possess it (Thuc. 1.70.8-9). [1] The Athenian *apragmones* would have seen the confirmation of this judgment in a Cleon. His activity, characterized above all in *Knights* as 'disturbance', was the opposite of hēsychia. 'Disturbance' was stormy and dark, [2] while hēsychia was calm and bright.

The opposition between brightness and darkness, as well as the other oppositions associated with it, are articulated in a fragment of Pindar (frag. 109 S-M), which can thus serve as the basis of a summary of the ideological issues under discussion.

τὸ κοινόν τιc ἀcτῶν ἐν εὐδίᾳ
τιθεὶc ἐρευναcάτω μεγαλάνοροc 'Ηcυχίαc τὸ φαιδρὸν φάοc,
cτάcιν ἀπὸ πραπίδοc ἐπίκοτον ἀνελών,
πενίαc δότειραν, ἐχθρὰν κουροτρόφου.

Let one set the commonality of the citizens in fine weather
and seek the bright light of proud Hēsychia
removing wrathful discord (*stasis*) from his mind,
discord the bestower of poverty, a hateful nurse of children.

The political order here desiderated is bathed in the light of Hēsychia, just like the new city that those Athenian *apragmones*, Euelpides and Peisthetairos, intended to found. The condition to be avoided is stasis, [3] which the central metaphors of *Knights* establish as the result of Cleon's activities. The fair weather [4] of the stasis-free city is the

---

[1] In Eur. *Suppl.*, Aethra, the mother of Theseus, wishes to persuade her son to take action on behalf of the mothers of those who fell in the expedition of the Seven against Thebes. She says that he should not be too cautious: 'Quiet (ἥcυχοι) cities, with their obscure deeds, also look obscure in their caution' (324-25).

[2] See Archilochus frag. 105 W and Gentili 1984:322-23, horizontal cols. 4 and 15.

[3] With the third of the lines quoted above, where *epikoton stasin* is to be removed from the mind, cf. *P.* 8.9-10: ὁπόταν τιc ἀμείλιχον/ καρδίᾳ κότον ἐνελάcῃ, where *kotos* has been nailed to the heart.

[4] εὐδία is contrasted with stormy weather in *P.* 5.10 and *I.* 7.38.

opposite of the storm that Cleon blows. [5] Finally, the impoverishment of the city caused by stasis (line 5 of the frag.) corresponds to Aristophanes' principal charge against Cleon, that he steals the city's money. [6]

Thucydides also regarded Cleon as a source of stasis. In 2.65.7, contrasting Pericles with his successors, the historian says that the latter acted κατὰ τὰς ἰδίας φιλοτιμίας καὶ ἴδια κέρδη. In the excursus on stasis, he says that all the ills arose διὰ πλεονεξίαν καὶ φιλοτιμίαν (3.82.8). From the death of Pericles, Athens, then, was already in a potential condition of stasis. The Mytilene Debate provides an illustration. Cleon suggests that Diodotus is κέρδει ἐπαιρόμενος (3.38.2), while Diodotus suggests, with implicit reference to Cleon, ἰδίᾳ τι αὐτῷ διαφέρει and goes on to say that slander (διαβαλών) is the means that such a person uses (3.42.2). [7] What Diodotus means is *philotimia*, selfish ambition. The Mytilene Debate thus articulates their opposition in terms the same as, or very similar to, the ones Thucydides uses to describe post-Periclean leadership and to analyze stasis. Like Cleon in *Knights*, Thucydides' Cleon is presented as a source of stasis. But the resemblance between the Aristophanic and the Thucydidean Cleons can be indicated more precisely, at the level of diction. The *first* two adjectives applied to Cleon in *Knights* are πανουργότατος and διαβολώτατος (45). The *final* words of Thucydides on Cleon, apropos his opposition to peace with Sparta, are: γενομένης ἡσυχίας καταφανέστερος νομίζων ἂν εἶναι κακουργῶν καὶ ἀπιστότερος διαβάλλων (5.16.1). Aristophanes and Thucydides are thus in complete agreement on the two main traits of Cleon: criminality (Ar.: πανουργότατος; Thuc.: κακουργῶν) and slander (Ar.: διαβολώτατος; Thuc.: διαβάλλων). Note that in Thucydides hēsychia is the opposite of the activities of Cleon, whose career, as I have suggested, is conceived by Thucydides in terms of stasis. In the context in Thucydides, hēsychia is stylistically an example of *variatio*, since εἰρήνη has just been used; but the stylistic function hardly precludes the deeper significance of the word, which here, as in Pindar and Aristophanes, indicates the opposite of stasis. [8] Compare also πιθανώτατος (Thuc. 3.36.6) and πιθανώτατα (*Eq.* 629). [9]

Pindar fr. 109 S-M thus provides in compact form the principal antitheses on which the portrait of Cleon in Aristophanes' *Knights* is built. If, however, these antitheses constitute an ideology linked to a minority of Dorian tastes and sympathies, a problem arises for the interpretation of *Knights*. How can Aristophanes effectively use this ideology as the basis of an attack on Cleon before an audience constituted of all sorts of citizens, the majority of whom presumably

---

[5] See section 2 above.
[6] With πενίας δότειραν, ἐχθρὰν κουροτρόφον cf. the epithets of Eirēnē, Hēsychia's aunt: τεθαλυῖαν (Hes. *Theog.* 901) and κουροτρόφος (Hes. *OD* 228).
[7] See LSJ⁹ s.v. διαφέρω III.2.
[8] Cf. the opposition at 8.71.1 between hēsychia and tarakhē (of the Athenian demos), presented, as one might expect, from the point of view of a Spartan; also, at 2.84.2-3 (of the Spartan fleet), where it is the viewpoint of the Athenian general, Phormio.
[9] For Cleon in Thuc. and Aristoph. see Kraus 1985:171-80.

did not espouse it? Is not *Knights* adopting a point of view that it would be difficult for them to share? One answer is suggested by an article by Donald Lateiner, [10] who studied "the man who does not meddle in politics" in the speeches of Lysias and showed that, in the law courts of the restored democracy, defendants typically stressed their *apragmosynē,* along with its associated virtues. A conclusion that might be drawn from this phenomenon, if it is not to be explained by a change in political involvement and the attitudes toward it between 430 and 380 B.C., [11] is that *apragmosynē* was a normal and unexceptionable position, one that could be respected by those who did not share it or had no reason for asserting it. Certainly the position of the gentlemen, of the 'sensible' ones, did not entail the claim that all others were *polypragmones* 'busybodies', only that some, like Cleon, were, and they could expect the demos to agree with them (cf. Ps.-Xen. 2.18).

In *Knights,* however, Aristophanes took special pains to weaken whatever connotation of social and economic class this ideology might possess. He did so in two ways: first by insinuating a rapprochement between the Knights and the demos, and second by providing an alternate ideology that could be shared by all Athenians. Before this rapprochement is discussed, the question of the relation of the contemporary ideology of hesychia (sections 3 and 4) to 'disturbance' in tradition (section 2) remains to be addressed.

---

[10] Lateiner 1982.
[11] Lateiner 1982:11-13 suggests that it is not. Cf., however, Connor 1971.

6. Stasis and Hēsychia (Theognis 39-52)

As is to be expected, the ideology of hēsychia derives from a traditional concept of the polis. Theognis 39-52 shows, in an almost schematic form, how the various aspects of the contemporary ideology discussed above are based on a traditional opposition between stasis and hēsychia:

Κύρνε, κύει πόλις ἥδε, δέδοικα δὲ μὴ τέκῃ ἄνδρα
εὐθυντῆρα κακῆς ὕβριος ἡμετέρης.   40
ἀστοὶ μὲν γὰρ ἔθ᾽ οἵδε σαόφρονες, ἡγεμόνες δὲ
τετράφαται πολλὴν εἰς κακότητα πεσεῖν.
οὐδεμίαν πω Κύρν᾽ ἀγαθοὶ πόλιν ὤλεσαν ἄνδρες·
ἀλλ᾽ ὅταν ὑβρίζειν τοῖσι κακοῖσι ἅδῃ,
δῆμόν τε φθείρωσι δίκας τ᾽ ἀδίκοισι διδῶσιν   45
οἰκείων κερδέων εἵνεκα καὶ κράτεος,
ἔλπεο μὴ δηρὸν κείνην πόλιν ἀτρεμίεσθαι,
μηδ᾽ εἰ νῦν κεῖται πολλῇ ἐν ἡσυχίῃ,
εὖτ᾽ ἂν τοῖσι κακοῖσι φίλ᾽ ἀνδράσι ταῦτα γένηται,
κέρδεα δημοσίῳ σὺν κακῷ ἐρχόμενα.   50
ἐκ τῶν γὰρ στάσιές τε καὶ ἔμφυλοι φόνοι ἀνδρῶν
μούναρχοί τε· πόλει μήποτε τῇδε ἅδοι.

Kyrnos, this polis is pregnant, and I fear lest it bear a man
to be a straightener of our base hybris.
The citizens here are still moderate, but the leaders
have veered so as to fall heavily into baseness.
Good men, Kyrnos, have never yet destroyed a polis;
but whenever it pleases the base to act with hybris
and they destroy the community and award judgments to the unjust
for the sake of private gain and power,
do not expect that polis to be calm for long,
not even if it now is set in abundant hēsychia,
whenever the base men take a liking to this:
private gains that bring harm to the community.
From these come stasis [plural], intestine murders,
and tyrants. May these things never be pleasing to this city.

In the situation here represented, the oligarchic leaders [1] through their hybris [2] have brought the city to the verge of stasis (51; cf. 1081-82),

---

[1] 40; the *kakoi* of 43 are also these leaders. See Nagy 1985:43-44.
[2] Cf. Pind. *P.* 8.12, discussed in section 4 above.

and its present condition of hēsychia (48) will be destroyed. [3] From stasis will emerge a tyrant: Theognis so intimates from the first with the oracular κύει, [4] and states explicitly at the end. [5] Stasis is also intimated at the outset in the opposition between 'straightener' (40) and 'veered' (41). [6] As the discussion of the ship-of-state metaphor showed, the positive principle underlying the metaphor is adherence to the straight and narrow. The fundamental situation of Theognis 39-52 is exactly the same as that pictured in the the ship-of-state metaphor; but, nearly bare of metaphoric language, Theognis' description names the specific hybristic acts of the leaders, unjust judgments, [7] which Hesiod calls 'crooked judgments'. [8] Indeed, Hesiod's application of the fable of the hawk and the nightingale, in an extended homily to Perses on the superiority of dikē over hybris, is another, more generalized articulation of the traditional ethical or political outlook under discussion here. Theognis also names the leaders' motives: private gain and power (46). The people, on the other hand, have remained cαόφρονεc (41). Sophrosynē is the ethical norm that the leaders have violated.

Theognis 39-52 show that the ideology based on hēsychia and sophrosynē and their related values is linked to the same fundamental political concept embodied in the ship-of-state metaphor. Theognis' poem can be taken as a matrix for the Cleon portrait in *Knights* in particular and in the other Aristophanic comedies in which Cleon is satirized, i.e., for the moral attitude shaping that portrait. [9] Cleon is a fomenter of stasis and a potential tyrant. He exhibits the same two motives Theognis attributes to the leaders of Megara—he is a thief, indeed a 'Charybdis of robbery' (*Eq.* 258) and he is power-hungry. In the allegory of the household in *Knights*, he is the steward of Demos, controlling Demos' affairs. The Sausage-seller competes for the position of steward, and the defeat of Paphlagon/Cleon is symbolized by his forfeiture of Demos' seal-ring (*Eq.* 947-59). In the leaders' unjust judgments, through which they seek private gain and power, the Theognidean poem provides the matrix for *Wasps*, to be discussed in section 9 below, in which Cleon is closely associated with a jury

---

[3] Cf. Pind. frag. 109 S-M, discussed in section 5 above, for the opposition between stasis and hēsychia.

[4] Cf. Hdt. 5.92β.3; 6.131.2. This sort of oracular response is parodied in *Eq.* 1037.

[5] 52 μούναρχοι. See Nagy 1985.44-45.

[6] Cf. the 'veering ways' (ἐκτραπέλοιcι νόμοιc) of the leaders at 290. Cf. Pind. *P.* 1.92, where, depending on the reading, the same adj. may apply to κέρδεα, i.e. there may be a very compressed form of the connection between 'veering' and private gain that we find in the poem of Theognis under discussion (cf. 42 with 46).

[7] Cf. the cessation of 'equitable division' (678) in Theognis' ship-of-state poem.

[8] *OD* 219, 221, cf. 224, 250, 258, 262, 264. A just speech, by contrast, would be 'straight': cf. Hom. *Il.* 18.508.

[9] And also, I believe, as the matrix for Thucydides' diagnosis of the ills of post-Periclean democracy in 2.65. See the comments on Thucydides in the preceding section of this monograph.

system represented as totally corrupt.

The poem is useful also in providing a sense of how Aristophanes could satirize Cleon on the comic stage from what might seem to us a point of view rather uncongenial to at least a part of his audience. At the end of the last section, I indicated the difficulties of Aristophanes' strategy. Theognis 39-52 show that the foundation of the ideology reflected in *Knights* is criticism of leadership. Theognis criticizes oligarchic leaders, but "[s]o universalized is this picture [of Megara] that the description of the emerging tyrant is expressed in words that would be appropriate for describing the Athenian lawgiver Solon in Solon's own poetry." [10] In *Knights*, Aristophanes can adopt the same critical stance toward a Cleon. He was not, however, content to rely on his audience's sympathetic reception of the traditional ideology as the basis of criticism of an Athenian leader. He also sought a rapprochement between contemporaries, i.e. the Knights, who might be most closely associated with this ideology, and the Athenian demos.

---

[10] Nagy 1985:43.

7. Rapprochement between the Knights and the Demos

      The rapprochement is effected in the epirrhematic syzygy in the parabasis. In the ode, the chorus of Knights appropriately invokes Poseidon, the god of horses, but, in keeping with a policy of conciliation on the part of the Knights, Poseidon is also invoked here as the god to whom 'pay-bringing triremes' are pleasing (555). These are the triremes that brought the annual tribute from the Athenian allies, which became the pay of the rowers and jurors. The cult-places with which Poseidon is associated in the ode are Sunium and Geraestus. Mention of Colonus, which was a cult-center of the Knights' Poseidon,[1] is not included. Poseidon is said to be 'dearest to Phormio, and, of all other gods, to the Athenians at present'. Phormio was "the type of the naval hero,"[2] and Poseidon must appear as his patron.

      The epirrhema (565-580) begins as a parody of that part of a funeral oration in which the ancestors are praised.[3] When the leader of the chorus speaks of 'our ancestors' as having fought 'battles on land and in the naval host', 'our' refers to all the Athenians, not to the Knights. They would not have remembered the history of their corps in terms of naval battles, and it is doubtful that the adjective translated 'on land' ($\pi\acute{\epsilon}\varsigma\alpha\iota c$), which suggests foot soldiers ($\pi\acute{\epsilon}\varsigma o\iota$), refers to their exploits. Reference to the historical fact of mounted hoplites[4] is excluded by the parodistic nature of the passage in any case,[5] but it is worth remembering that the Athenian Knights kept a separate identity. Gomme has observed: ". . .the social change which followed the military reorganization (in the 6th century probably) by which the nobility in all Greek states entered the phalanx of hoplites and so tended to lose their separate status, was by no means so complete at Athens as at Sparta. . . .Just as, in spite of Salamis and the radical democracy, the hoplites preserved their social as well as their military distinction, so did the nobility survive, and its status, or at least its wealth, was recognized by the institution of cavalry."[6] In confirmation of Gomme's observation, *IG* I^{2}946 (restored from *AP*

---

[1] Siewert 1979:280-289.
[2] Neil 1901 on 562.
[3] See Ziolkowski 1981:74-100 for the topos.
[4] Greenhalgh 1973.
[5] A few lines later, in 595-610, the horses are praised in terms that would be appropriate to their masters, as Loraux has observed. See Appendix on 595-610.
[6] *HCT* 1:328.

7.254) shows that the Knights would commemorate their horseman-ship; and it is notable that after the battles of Corinth and Coronea in 394 B. C. the Knights set up their own monument and casualty-list, [7] while the other casualties were recorded by tribe on the official list. [8]

'Our ancestors' did not include Knights. [9] The army is divided into land and naval forces but no further distinction is made. The past was a time of harmony. Further, the old-time general did not demand free meals in the prytaneum or the privilege of a front seat (573-76). The speaker alludes to the privileges received by Cleon after his success at Pylos (cf. 702-704). The speaker concludes the epirrhema by stating the noble claims of the Knights in implied con-trast to those of Cleon. The Knights ask only to defend the city and its gods, without recompense, and, after the war is over, to wear their hair long and scrape themselves with the strigil after exercise (576-80). [10]

In the antode, the chorus invokes Athena. This Athena is peculiar in two ways. First, she is associated with poetry, as were the Athenians themselves in the kommation (504-506). She brings Victory, the companion of choristers (589); she protects a city 'mighty in war and poets' (583-84; cf. again 504-506). The patroness of Athens is expected to be the patroness of this chorus (592) and to bring victory to the play in the dramatic competition. This comic imposture is only intensified by the second peculiarity of the antode.

The Athena invoked by the chorus was a popular deity, [11] and, for this reason, the goddess whom Cleon liked to call upon. As *Knights* shows, Cleon was an "Athenist" [12] and he may have had something to do with the construction of the temple of Athena Nikē. [13] The epithet used of Athena here, $\mu\epsilon\delta\acute{\epsilon}o\nu\varsigma\alpha$ 'protecting', (585) is one

---

[7] Tod, *GHI*, vol. 2, no. 104 (*IG* ii²5222).
[8] See discussion by Tod, *ibid.* (preceding note).
[9] There may be just a hint of the Knights in that old-time Athens in the reference to the *peplos* in 565. The Knights participated in the procession in which the *peplos* was borne up to the acropolis at the Panathenaea. Alföldi 1967, combining his interpretation of Hdt. 6.112 with an imprecise reading of *Knights* 595ff., states: "Nicht ohne Berechtigung rühmen sich die Ritter im Jahr 424 bei Aristophanes ihrer Heldentaten zu Pferd, zu Fuss, und zur See." Neither in 595ff. nor in 565ff. do we have cavalry fighting as infantry or hoplites.
[10] See Donlan 1980:157.
[11] See Nilsson 1955:439-40, citing Sophocles, frag. 760 N for her *Volkstümlichkeit*, and Herington 1963. For problems in the evidence for private dedications to Athena, see Mikalson 1983:115-116.
[12] 652-56, 763-64, 1090-91, 1171-72, 1177, 1181-82.
[13] As Welsh 1978:250-79 argues, starting with a suggestion of Boersma 1970:84-86. See also Meiggs 1972:496-503. As Zimmermann 1985:208 observes, mention of Athena and Nikē in the same context would inevitably remind the audience of the statue of Athena Parthenos, which represents Athena with Nikē in her hand (cf. *Eq.* 1169-76).

that Cleon will later use when he parodies the opening of the Themistocles decree (763-64)[14] as part of his assimilation of himself to Themistocles (811-12). The epithet was, however, no longer in use in Athens; it was an East Greek cult-title related to the religious or politico-religious policy of Athens toward its allies in the Delian League. [15] The Knights are thus appropriating Cleon's imperialist Athena and associating her with their own goal of victory in the dramatic competition. As in the ode they presented Poseidon in an agreeable democratic light, so in the antode they seek to appropriate the city's patroness for their own ends and at the same time to preempt Cleon's "Athenism."

The antepirrhema praises the Knights' horses for bravely leaping into the transport ships (599) and behaving like true sailors (600-603). The reference is to the Knights' participation in Nicias' campaign on the Isthmus (Thuc. 4.42-44), where they had played a part in the victory at Solygeia (Thuc. 4.44.1; cf. *Eq.* 266-69, which may refer to their success). The speaker can thus praise the Knights in an agreeable fashion by assimilating horses to sailors. He also quotes Theorus, the associate of Cleon, as quoting a 'Corinthian crab' on the Knights' achievement, and, through this complicated joke, makes the Knights' enemies within Athens admit their effectiveness. [16]

In the parabasis, then, Aristophanes finds ways to bring either himself or the Knights together with the nautical activity of the Athenian lower class, [17] and it is incorrect to speak of this parabasis as one that steers clear of the issues of the play. [18]

---

[14] For the text, see Jameson 1960:198-223.

[15] Barron 1964:35-48 refers to "colonisation propaganda." The main subject of this article are *horoi*, boundary-stones, of *temene* of Athena, Ἀθηνῶν μεδέουcα, and of the Eponymoi and Ion (both Ἀθήνηθεν), found in Samos. Barron argues that they are of Samian workmanship and of East Greek wording, including Athena's cult-title. The *horos* from Kos (reference in n. 46) proves that the cult-title was not peculiar to Samos. The headquarters of the cult was Athens: that is the meaning of Ἀθήνηθεν. (Cf. Smyth, *GG* 1661.) "The only hypothesis which will meet the case is of a series of common League cults voluntarily set up at the suggestion of the members of the Delian League, and having their headquarters at Athens. The inclusion of Ion and the Eponymoi is a reference to the tradition that all Ionia was settled from Athens at the end of the period of the Dorian invasions. An obvious suggestion would be that the cults were initiated at the same time as the League itself" (p. 45; for other possibilities for the date of the Samian *horoi*, see n. 83). See also Meiggs 1972:295-98 and Alty 1982:1-14, especially 8-11, for the negative side of Ionianism and Cassio 1985: ch. 10 ("Atene Madrepatria degli Ioni: la 'Pace' e il Dramma Contemporaneo") for the ambiguous attitude of comedy toward the Ionians (jokes reflecting negative popular opinion of the Ionians; defense of them as allies, especially in the anti-imperialist perspective of comedy).

[16] See Appendix on 608-10.

[17] See Dover 1972:99.

[18] Halliwell 1984a:17 n. 24.

8. Alternate Ideology

The alternate ideology is expressed in the last scene. [1] In the last scene of *Knights,* Demos reappears on stage after undergoing a magical beauty treatment. Although he has been made beautiful instead of ugly (1321), he has been as much transported as transformed. Despite what is often assumed about this transformation, Demos, formerly in this play an old man, is still an old man. [2] The place to which he has been transported is the old Athens (1323, 1327), which was 'sleek and violet-crowned' (1329). Demos is thus rejuvenated in the sense that he has become an old man in an earlier, better Athens, or, in terms of the personification, he is the Athenian demos before it was corrupted. On stage there was some sort of revelation—the mechanics elude us—of the old Athens, in particular of the Acropolis (1326-27). [3]

Demos now wears a golden cricket in his hair. It is an ornament that older men wore in the days of the Persian Wars. Thucydides mentions the custom, along with the linen chiton, as evidence of the soft-living (τὸ ἁβροδίαιτον) of the older men of that time (1.6.3). He says that it is not long since the custom was abandoned. [4] Thucydides' testimony alone does not confirm the relation of the cricket to maturity, but in the absence of any evidence to the contrary (with the apparent exception of line 1349) Demos' cricket must be taken as a sign that he is an old man and that the Sausage-seller's account of what he has done to Demos is exhaustive: 'I have boiled him down and have made him beautiful instead of ugly' (1321). Demos' attitude is that of an older man. He complains of the 'youth' (1375 μειράκια) in the agora, just as Stronger Argument, another Aristophanic old man, addresses Pheidippides as a 'youth' (990 μειράκιον) and tells him that he will learn to hate the agora (991; cf. Isoc. 7.48).

---

[1] For a survey of the literary-critical problem, see Landfester 1967:83ff.

[2] To anticipate a possible objection to this point, I should like to say that I do not take line 1349 to mean 'Was I that stupid and senile'? (Sommerstein 1981), i.e. that he is now young, not old and senile. The participle ὤν is understood with καὶ γέρων and the line thus means: 'Was I that stupid, though I was an old man (and should have known better)'? For the association of old age and wisdom, cf. Hes. *Th.* 234; Hom. *Od.* 2.16, 3.19-20, 4.204-205.

[3] See Appendix on 1326-34.

[4] Vase paintings confirm that the custom died out in the 470s: *HCT* 1:102. (Cf. n. 9 below for the cricket as passé.)

The transformation of Demos is indicated by three other signs in addition to the golden cricket. First, he is radiant in the old-style dress (1331), presumably the linen chiton of which Thucydides spoke. Second, he is redolent of peace. [5] Third, he is annointed with myrrh (1332). [6] In this form, he is greeted by the Knights as faring in a fashion worthy of 'the trophy at Marathon' (1334). [7] The Marathon generation, then, in addition to its famous toughness, has another side. This generation is not only tough, it is soft. [8] Demos is even assigned other appurtenances of the old-time luxury—a portable stool on which to sit wherever he may happen to be (1384; cf Athen. 12.512C) and a boy to carry it (1385). If Demos wishes, he can use the boy as a stool, too (1386). In other words, he is invited to enjoy some good old-fashioned buggery. [9]

Aristophanes has not invented the softness of the Marathon generation. The parallel between Aristophanes and Thucydides in the matter of the golden cricket has already been mentioned. Athough the evidence for the softness of this generation is not as extensive as for its toughness, it seems that the former was as well known as the latter. Two fragments of Old Comedy, one from Teleclides (frag. 215 K) and one from Cratinus (frag. 86 K), speak of the luxury of the time of Themistocles, i.e. the time of the Persian Wars. It is not a matter of those images of *Schlaraffenland* in which Old Comedy abounded [10] but a concept of a particular historical period, which, in these examples, is tied to the name of Themistocles. [11] Although it is not immediately clear why, the Athenians prided themselves on the softness of their forebears, and the Periclean Funeral Oration (Thuc. 2.35-46) shows that the generation of the Peloponnesian War was proud to maintain the tradition. Pericles implicitly contrasts Athens with the Doric Sparta, which lives by the rule of all work and no play. In Athens, says Pericles, we have many festivals. We have handsome

---

[5] Neil 1901 on 1332: "There is of course the common play on both meanings of σπονδαί, peace and festal libation, the second meaning leading on to the mention of festal array."

[6] Compare another set of indices of the soft-living of this generation in Cratinus, *Chirones* frag. 239 K (from Athen. 553E): a staff, an apple, mint, and flowers.

[7] See Ehrenberg 1935: ch. V ("Die Generation von Marathon").

[8] Sommerstein 1981 on 1334 observes: "Cf. *Wasps* 711 where Bdelycleon, in almost the same words, claims that these same achievements ought to be rewarded by giving all Athenians a life of luxury at others' expense."

[9] Compare Right (or Stronger) Speech in *Clouds*. Much of his discussion of the 'old-time education' (961) has to do with pederasty. His opponent, referring to the cricket custom (984), chides him as passé. Right replies: But this was the education that produced the Marathonomachae (985-86). Philokleon, the old man in *Wasps*, enjoys looking at boys' genitals at their *dokimasia* (578).

[10] Athen. 6.267E-270A collects the passages. The central theme of *Schlaraffenland* is the easy availability of food.

[11] The contradiction between the two concepts was commented on in the fourth century B.C. by Heraclides Ponticus, who drew upon the passages in Thucydides and in *Knights* I have already discussed (Athen. 12.512C).

private dwellings (2.38.1) that give us pleasure. We do not go in for strict child-rearing but are relaxed (2.39.1). We love beauty (2.40.1). Our citizens are graceful and dexterous (2.41.1). And yet we are not soft (2.40.1); we are brave fighters when circumstances demand (2.39.2-4). [12]

To return to Demos in the last scene of *Knights*: does his new luxuriousness have this same point? Yes, but in a more precise and sinister form. The contrast between Athens and Sparta as presented by Pericles is the contrast between an Ionian and a Doric city. Ionia, the Eastern part of the Greek world, was supposed to have been colonized by Athens. This tradition is as early as Solon, who speaks of Athens as the 'eldest land of Ionia'. [13] In the aftermath of the Persian Wars, the Ionian Greeks appealed to Athens, on the basis of kinship, to assume the leadership (Thuc. 1.95.1; and so was formed the Delian League: 1.96). In the time of Thucydides and Aristophanes, however, this traditional idea had been given an ideological twist. From the mid-fifth century, that is from the time when Athens moved the treasury of the Delian league from Delos to Athens and became a frankly imperial city, Athens began to use the Ionian connection for propaganda purposes. [14] Athens' East Greek allies, or subjects, are bound to her not just by the annual tribute they are forced to pay but also by their filial status as colonies. At first, Athens awarded her colonies a privileged status amongst the allies by allowing (i.e. forcing) them to contribute an ox and a panoply to the Panathenaia and to march in the procession. By the time, however, of the great reassessment of tribute in 425/4 B.C., which took place shortly before the production of *Knights,* it became convenient to confer this status on *all* the allies. [15] The groundwork had been laid by Pericles, who encouraged the belief that the Athens and the cities of the Delian League were *homophyloi* (Thuc. 1.141.6). [16] One could give several further examples of this "colonisation propaganda," [17] but enough has been said to put the question of Demos in focus.

Demos is characterized in fact not just as one of the luxurious old men of the Marathon age but also specifically as an Ionian. The golden cricket is the sign. In the passage in Thucydides already discussed (1.6.3), it is said that the older men amongst the Ionians wore the golden cricket for a long time because of their kinship with the Athenians. Whether or not Thucydides is right about the

[12] Cf. the notion of 'gentleness' (τὸ μαλθακόν) in Pind. *P.* 8 (section 4 above).
[13] Frag. 4a.2 W; cf. Hdt. 5.97, 9.106; Thuc. 7.57.4. There is probably a kernel of truth in the idea: see Graham 1983:11 n.2.
[14] See Barron 1964.
[15] *ATL* 1.155, ll.57-8.
[16] See Culham 1978:29-30.
[17] For the evidence for this propaganda see Barron 1964:46-48. One could perhaps add the Ionic Athena Nike temple: Boersma 1970:75-76.

direction of the influence, [18] there can be no doubt that it was a shared custom, and, if in Ionia it signified Athens, in Athens it signified Ionia. [19] Old Demos has, then, become an Ionian. Or rather he has become an Athenian of the period in which—so Aristophanes pretends—Athenian and Ionian were still the same thing. In this period, things that are now separate and irreconcilable come together: virtue and pleasure, to begin with. Demos can be luxurious and, at the same time, he is the Demos who dined with Miltiades and Aristides (1325).

One might have expected Themistocles to be named here, just as he is synonymous with the good old days in the fragments of Telecleides and Cratinus cited above. In the course of *Knights* both Cleon (763-64, 811-12) and the enemies of Cleon (83) have emulated Themistocles, and now, with the Sausage-seller's triumphant recreation of Demos, it would seem that the question of who is the new Themistocles has been decided. That question is dropped, however, and two other illustrious personages from the days of the Persian Wars are named as the dinner companions of Demos. Of these two, one, Aristeides, needs no explanation. He was "the Just" (cf. Hdt. 8.79.1), and, if anyone, should be mentioned in this context. The other, Miltiades, is more difficult. From soon after the Persian Wars, Miltiades and Themistocles became ideological antitypes, the one standing for the naval victory at Salamis, the other for the hoplite victory at Marathon. [20] Stesimbrotus wrote that it was by overcoming the opposition of Miltiades that Themistocles was able to build a fleet (Plut. *Themist.* 24.5=*FGrH*2B107F*3). In *Knights*, with its gesture of reconciliation toward the rowers, one might have expected that Themistocles would be mentioned in the final scene. And yet it is the hoplite general Miltiades who is mentioned, and the Knights call Demos 'worthy of the trophy at Marathon' (1334). Mention of Themistocles might have been omitted because his character was suspect, [21] and oligarchs could use his exile as an example of the demos' fickleness. [22] In any case, Aristophanes had positive reasons for naming Miltiades as one of Demos' companions. As will be argued shortly, Aristophanes wished to present the renewed Demos as incorporating and thus transcending the contemporary ideological and political divisions with Athens. To this end, a pairing of the oligarchs' hero and Demos is quite appropriate. Furthermore, the naval policy of Themistocles is tacitly reaffirmed in the final scene. Faced with the decision whether to spend money on triremes or on direct pay to the citizens, Demos will build triremes (1350-55), just as Themistocles in his day, when the Athenians were faced with the same decision, had caused them to build a fleet with the income from the silver mines at Laureum (Hdt.

---

[18] Gomme thinks that Thucydides has it backwards: the Athenians wore the golden cricket because of the Ionians.

[19] Asius frag. 13 Kinkel (a quotation in Douris *FGrH*76F60 from Athen. 12.525E-F) seems to connect the custom of the cricket with Samos. Survey of the problem of the cricket in Gomme on Thuc. 1.6.3. The evidence is set out by Cook 1940:250-56.

[20] Loraux 1973:25.

[21] Timocreon, *PMG* 727 from Plut. *Themist.* 21. With the food imagery of the last stanza, cf. *Eq.* 814-816.

[22] So I interpret Andocides frag. 3. Cf. Thucydides' comment on the fickleness of the demos in relation to Pericles.

7.144). As for his new administrative policy, the first item on Demos' list is pay for the rowers (1365-66, cf. 1065-66). Demos, then, is both the companion of the hoplite general and the continuator of the policies of the founder of the Athenian navy.

Again, city and country. Demos now returns to the country (1394) but he continues his attendance in the assembly and in the law courts (1350-53; 1358-61). Again, the most striking example of all, war and peace. The new Demos of the Marathonian Athens makes peace with Sparta (1388-94) but keeps Athens on a war footing (1366-71).

Disarmament is unthinkable if Demos is not only the 'monarch of this land' (1330) but also 'king of the Greeks' (1333). [23] In the reconstituted Athens, none of Cleon's imperialism, about which Aristophanes always seems so bitter, is given up: a first major concession on Aristophanes' part. The soft-but-tough Ionian Athens is the imperial city in its pristine form.

What would be the fate of the Knights, Aristophanes' sponsors, in this city? Has Aristophanes found a place for them? The Knights have disappeared. [24] Instead of their long hair, we now have the Ionian bun held up by the golden cricket. [25] Pederasty, identified with the Knight's class in Aristophanes' time, [26] is now available to Demos (1384-86). It was part of the good old days (1387). Anointed with myrrh and redolent of wine, Demos looks like a symposiast (cf. 1325: he is now the one who dined with Aristeides and Miltiades). Another characteristic activity of the Knights has been opened to Demos. [27] In sum, as the Sausage-seller announces when he first presents the new Demos, 'I have made him *kalos*' (1321). The unthinkable has happened. As the Old Oligarch makes abundantly clear, the people are by definition immune to beauty and unbeautiful.

The Knights are thus ellipsed in the new equation of softness and toughness. This ellipsis is the final form of the reconciliation proposed in the parabasis. On the side of toughness, the new Athens is internally busy, political, and, toward the world, imperialist. The Knights' apolitical values do not have a chance. On the side of softness, the new Athens, in recovering its Ionian style, simply renders negligible the Knights' prerogatives in the area of beauty. Now everyone can be beautiful.

---

[23] Cf. the notion of the tyrant city in Pericles' third speech in Thucydides (2.63), which Thucydides presents not as a private meditation but as a speech before the Athenian people. Cleon continues the theme (Thuc. 3.37).

[24] Cf. Strauss 1966:105, 107-108.

[25] Ehrenberg 1951:97 did not realize that there is a significant difference in the two hair styles.

[26] Ehrenberg 1951:100.

[27] Ehrenberg 1951:103 on the symposium.

In order to achieve the defeat of Cleon, Aristophanes has had to concede much. He even seems to betray his friends (n.b. 507-11), the Knights. Ironically, their own picture of the good old days, when there were only the navy and the foot-soldiers, has become a reality. Aristophanes has had to sacrifice them in order to create an Athens in which there would be no Cleon.

One can be more precise about what he sacrifices in the Knights. When the Knights are first mentioned, they are called ἀγαθοί (225), whereas there is another group of Athenians who are καλοί τε κἀγαθοί (227, cf. 185, 738), distinguished, furthermore, from those in the audience who are 'clever' (228; is there the implication that the kaloi te kagathoi are not even in the audience?). The boiled-down Demos, for his part, is καλός (1321), but not, apparently, agathos. Demos has the good looks of a gentleman but nothing more. The play replaces one virtue, the Knights', indicated by ἀγαθοί, with another, Demos', indicated by καλός. Aristophanes assumes that the Athenians will give up Cleon if they can be kaloi, and on these terms he will sacrifice the virtue of the Knights. Whatever happened to the kaloi te kagathoi, those who possess the complete virtue of which the Knights and Demos each have a part? They are not considered. There is no Athens for them. (What the Sausage-seller says at 736-40, where he compares Demos to a fickle boy who rejects lovers who are kaloi te kagathoi, remains true.) It is possible that Aristophanes mentions them only to distinguish the Knights from them. [28] If Aristophanes considers the Knights only agathoi, not kaloi te kagathoi, it is easier to see why he is willing to make them laughable in this play and to abandon them at the end.

The final scene of Knights, then, presents an ideology alternate to that of hēsychia and sōphrosynē, values that might have been too closely linked with the class represented by the Knights. For that matter, the final scene even replaces the Knights with a renewed Demos, i.e., with a political order in which the Knights are unnecessary. The days of the ancestors of whom they spoke in the parabasis have indeed returned. In this way, the defeat of Cleon, who is most persuasive to the people (629; Thuc. 3.36.6), is made more acceptable. Further, Aristophanes makes the new order of things acceptable by making it continuous, in important respects, with the policies of Cleon. In particular, the new Demos, as 'king of the Greeks' (1333), continues the imperialism of Cleon. Earlier intimations of Ionian propaganda in the play are now realized in a fully Ionian or Ionicized Demos.

At the same time, the final scene is also the final

---

[28] The Knights should, however, have been called kaloi te kagathoi. That would have been normal. See Deinarchus 3.12 and the comment of de Ste. Croix 1972:372; Ehrenberg 1951:95.

achievement of the policy of 'disturbance' proposed to the Sausage-seller by the Knights, a policy which meant to make mincemeat of the city's affairs (213-15; quoted above in section 1). The decoction of Demos has a mythical prototype, in which the victim is chopped into pieces before he is boiled down. Pelias underwent this procedure at the hands of his daughters or of Medea (Diod. 4.52.3; Paus. 8.11.3). Paradoxically, the ultimate 'disturbance' recreates the city. The reappearance of Demos is an epiphany, [29] and it may be that the second parabasis, usually considered a rather inorganic part of the play, sets the mood for the epiphany. Now that the Sausage-seller has won his final victory over Cleon, who has been banished to the edge of the city, the Knights exult. In their second parabasis, the strophe parodies a Pindaric prosodion, [30] and although to us the form seems to have nothing to do with the content, and although the obscenity of the first epirrhema (1274-89) seems gratuitous, the effect may have been, like the banishment of Cleon, purificatory [31] and celebratory. [32]

---

[29] Kleinknecht 1939:58-65.
[30] Dale 1968:180.
[31] Note the curse (1288-89), with which cf. Eupolis *Demoi* frag. 1.33ff. and the remarks of Kraus 1985:159-60.
[32] Already in antiquity, the second parabasis was a problem. It was believed that it was the work of Eupolis: see schol. *Nub.* 540; schol. *Eq.* 1291. These scholia should be placed in the context of allegations and counter-allegations by Aristophanes, Cratinus, and Eupolis concerning *contaminatio*. See Perusino 1981:407-413.

9. Cleon in *Wasps*

In *Knights,* Aristophanes gets rid of Cleon, even if Athens, electing him shortly after the performance one of the ten generals for 424/3 B.C., did not. In *Clouds* of the following year (423 B.C.), Aristophanes refers to Cleon by his slave name, Paphlagon (cf. *Pax* 314), chiding the Athenians for the election (*Nub.* 581-94). Aristophanes is proud of having attacked Cleon when he was at the height of his power and also of having refrained when Cleon was down (*Nub.* 549-50; the reference to restraint is unclear). In 422 B.C. in *Wasps,* Aristophanes begins by saying that he has abandoned the attack, and readers of this comedy have tended to believe him. [1] A reading of the play attentive to Cleon, however, shows that the attack continues, as, for that matter it does in *Peace* of the following year, even after Cleon is dead. [2] Indeed, *Wasps* is in this respect continuous with *Knights* and with the statements in *Clouds* concerning the election of Cleon. Not only is *Wasps* continuous with *Knights* as an attack on Cleon, it is continuous both in the aspects of Cleon that are attacked and in Aristophanes' handling of the ideological issues. A study of Cleon in *Wasps* corroborates the interpretation of *Knights* that I have offered.

At 54, Xanthias turns to the audience and tells them the subject of the play. He begins with a list of things the audience should not expect. One of these is abuse of Cleon. 'We shall not again make mincemeat (verb μυττωτεύω; cf. *Eq.* 771) of the same man, if thanks to luck Cleon has shown forth' (62-63). [3] 'Not again' refers to *Knights* of two years earlier, in which Cleon appeared as the Paphlagonian steward of Demos, and the luck to which Xanthias refers is most naturally taken as Cleon's success at Pylos, which was ridiculed again and again in *Knights.* [4] Lines 62-63 mean: 'Two years ago, Cleon had a stroke of luck, his success at Pylos, and we made mincemeat of him. We shall not do so again'. In *Wasps,* Aristophanes keeps Xanthias' promise, at least to the extent that he does not introduce Cleon as a character in the play, except as the dog of

---

[1] MacDowell 1971:2, while recognizing the anti-Cleon tendency of the play, states: "But *Wasps* is not just about Kleon. . . .The main object of attack is rather the legal system which facilitated unfair prosecutions and convictions." Cf. Rose 1960:234: *Wasps* "is a satire on the jury-system of Athens. . ."

[2] *Pax* 47-48, 268-73, 313-21, 647-56, 752-60 ~ *Vesp.* 1030-37.

[3] Thucydides considered Cleon's success at Pylos a matter of luck (5.7.3, and consider the theme of *tukhē* in the narrative of the Pylos episode).

[4] 54-57, 391-94, 469, 702, 709, 742-43, 766, 843-46, 1052-61, 1166-67, 1201.

Kydathenaion in the domestic trial scene (891-1008). Whether he refrains from mincing Cleon is another question. At the time he makes this promise, Xanthias has already interpreted the dream of his fellow slave, Sosias, in such a way that it unmistakably refers to Cleon. Sosias said (31-36):

> In the early part of the night I thought I saw on the Pnyx
> sheep huddled together in the Assembly
> with walking sticks and cloaks.
> And then I thought that to these sheep a devouring [5]
> whale delivered a harangue
> with the voice of a blazing sow. [6]

Xanthias interrupts Sosias, telling him that his dream smells of rotten leather (37-38), i.e. of Cleon, mocked already as a tanner in *Knights* (44 and schol. 892) and already ridiculed for his inferior product (315-21) and his loud voice. [7] Sosias' dream has two more details, both of which are again essentially a replay of anti-Cleon satire in *Knights*. First, the repulsive (adj. μιαρός; cf. *Eq.* 329, 823, 831) whale had a pair of scales with which she began to weight some beef-fat (39-40). Xanthias takes δημός 'fat' as δῆμος 'people' (cf. *Eq.* 954) and says that the whale intends to divide the people (cf. *Eq.* 817-18). Second, Theorus, with the head of a crow, was sitting near her on the ground. This element of the dream is developed in such a way as to make fun of Theorus as the flatterer of Cleon (42-46, cf. *Eq.* 608, where Theorus would not have been introduced if he were not an associate of Cleon). Sosias' dream, then, is a recapitulation of the Cleon-portrait of *Knights*—the loud-mouthed upstart divisive coercive tanner demagogue with his flatterer Theorus—and Aristophanes has already done to some extent what Xanthias promises the play will not do.

Does Aristophanes keep the promise *after* Xanthias has made it? The answer to this question depends upon the relation, in the rest of the play, between the plot and reference to Cleon. If references to Cleon are in the nature of one-liners and the plot has little or nothing to do with Cleon, then Xanthias can be taken at his word in 62-63. If, however, abuse of Cleon is more fundamental and pervasive, Xanthias' disclaimer—'we shall not make mincemeat of Cleon'—is a kind of dramatic *praeteritio*. He denies a theme in order to announce

---

[5] Kraus 1985:192 argues that πανδοκεύτρια should be understood as 'hostess'. Cf. Glauketes, the glutton (*Pax* 1008; Plato frag. 106 K), as κῆτος 'whale' at *Thesmo.* 1037.

[6] Or a 'singed sow', alluding, like the smell of leather, to Cleon's profession? Cf. *Eq.* 1236, where the Sausage-seller says that he was educated in singeing pits. Kraus 1985:192 argues for a literal interpretation, saying that, during the Spartan invasions of Attica, pigs would often have been burnt alive in their pens.

[7] 137, 256, 274-76, cf. 217, 286, 304, 311, 487, 626, 863, 1018, 1023, 1403. As Kraus 1985:173 observes, *Eq.* echoes from beginning to end with Cleon's shouting.

it.

The plot of the comedy concerns the attempt of a son to cure his father of a mania for jury duty and to introduce him to a more pleasant and refined way of life. Unable to cure him, the son must forcibly confine his father in their house. The old man's fellow-jurors come to summon him to the day's activities. The old man attempts to escape and nearly succeeds. The old jurors enter into a brawl with the son and his slaves. Finally, father and son agree to a debate on the advantages of jury-duty. The son successfully argues that, far from conferring advantages, the system exploits the jurors. The cronies of the old man are persuaded but he is not. To indulge his father's unremitting passion for the jury courts, the son puts on a private trial at home. When the time for voting comes, he tricks his father into voting for acquittal, and this involuntary act marks the end of the old man's days as a juror. In the second half of the play, after the main parabasis, he changes his old mania for new ones. [8]

The names of the father and of the son are significant. The father, whose ruling passion is jury-duty, is Philocleon 'Love-Cleon'. The son, who exposes the system as fraudulent and who changes his father's way of life, is Bdelycleon 'Loathe-Cleon'. Although the names are used sparingly after they are first announced by Xanthias (133-34) [9] and although the audience may have thought of the two characters as the old man and the young man, [10] the fact remains that the very announcement of the names, which comes, remarkably, before the appearance of the characters themselves, [11] links the names and thus Cleon thematically with the plot and thus with the issue of the jury system.

This link has a historical basis, if Cleon was responsible for raising the jurors' pay to three obols per day a few years before *Wasps* (schol. Rav. *V.* 88, schol. *Av.* 1541). In *Wasps*, in any case, the jurors look to Cleon as their champion, just as in *Knights*, Paphlagon/Cleon, under attack by the chorus of horsemen, calls upon the jurors for aid: ὦ γέροντες ἡλιασταί, φράτερες Τριωβόλου 'old jurymen, brothers of the three-obol guild'. [12] In *Wasps*, when the old juryman Philocleon is confined in his house by his son, Bdelucleon 'Loathe-Cleon', he calls upon Cleon and his fellow-jurors for aid: ὦ ξυνδικασταὶ καὶ Κλέων, ἀμύνατε 'Fellow-jurors and Cleon, help me'! (197). It is the first mention of the chorus, which has not yet appeared on stage. When the

---

[8] On the relation of the two halves (which are not, to be sure, the same size), see Schwinge 1975a:35-47.
[9] Bdelucleon: 137, 372; Philocleon: 163, 1466.
[10] See MacDowell 1971:149 on 134.
[11] Dover 1972:128.
[12] 255, cf. 51. They are old men in this play as in *Wasps*. Cf. *Eq.* 210 and frag. adesp. 11 K (from Plut. *Nic.* 2.3), where Cleon is described as γεροντᾱγᾱγῶν.

old jurors are about to enter into combat with Bdelycleon and his slaves, they send their sons for Cleon (409-411):

> report this to Cleon
> and bid him come
> against an enemy of the city. . .

They later call Cleon their κηδεμών 'protector' (242). In arguing the advantages of the jurors, Philocleon says (596-97):

> Cleon himself, the shout-conqueror, leaves us alone unbitten; rather, he protects and keeps hold of us and shoos the flies away.

Philocleon goes on to mention the flattering attention the jurors receive from Cleon's stooge, Theorus (599-600), whom the jurors have earlier called their champion (418). [13] If the jurors identify so closely with Cleon, why do they use the name Demologocleon 'Soapbox-Cleon' [14] to vilify Bdelycleon (342)—and in a context in which they show that they suspect him of being an enemy of the people (344-45)? In their spluttering indignation, they unintentionally abuse one of their own supporters, as they do elsewhere. [15]

What is here a Freudian slip on the part of the jurors becomes a matter of consciousness both for them and for Philocleon after the main agon, when they are persuaded they are the dupes of thievish politicians and in particular of Cleon. Although Philocleon is unable to give up his passion for jury-duty, the lyric dialogue between father and son concluding the main agon ends with the old man's threat: 'In that case, may I never in the future, when I'm in court, find Cleon guilty of theft', (758-59) meaning, 'or he'll get it'! Although Bdelycleon did not mention any politician by name in the agon, Philocleon knows who was meant. After hearing the agon, the old jurors are ready to exchange Cleon as protector for someone like Bdelycleon 'Loathe-Cleon': 'Would that I had some kinsman or protector (κηδεμών; cf. 242) to give me such advice' (731-32). [16]

Embezzlement, one of Bdelycleon's main charges against

---

[13] Cf. 42-43, discussed in the text above, 1220, 1236-37.

[14] To use MacDowell's apt rendering.

[15] Thus Sommerstein ad loc., who compares 418 (Theorus) and 592 (Cleonymus).

[16] The particular allegation of accepting bribes from the allied cities (669-71) had been used by the Sausage-seller against Paphlagon/Cleon in *Eq.* 801-802 (cf. 930-33); and in Thucydides the Mytileneans in 428 B.C. say that they have courted the Athenian public and its leaders, implying bribery of the latter: ἀπὸ θεραπείας τοῦ τε κοινοῦ. . .καὶ τῶν αἰεὶ προεστώτων (3.11.7). There seems to be a slight zeugma, since the *therapeia* would have taken two different forms. The irony is that Cleon was immune to the Mytileneans' overtures, if they made any to him.

the politicians, returns in the domestic trial scene. The dog of Kydathenaion, representing Cleon, prosecutes the dog Labes, representing Laches. [17] This scene seems to be a comic anticipation of the trial of Laches which Cleon had announced, according to the old jurors, for the next day (240-44), a trial about which nothing else is known. The comic prosecution of Laches by Cleon, however, displayed one of the main political and ideological oppositions of the day—the gentleman soldier [18] vs. the upstart tanner, the peace-maker [19] vs. the war-monger (Thuc. 5.16.1). Unable to speak in his own defense, Labes/Laches is just like the old aristocrat Thucydides the son of Melesias (944-49, cf. *Ach.* 703-12). The dog of Kydathenaion frankly admits that part of the reason for his prosecution is that Labes/Laches did not give him a share of the embezzlement (914-16). The defendant must be convicted because 'one bush could never feed two thieves' (927-28)—Athens is not big enough for both of them. The dog of Kydathenaion goes on to say that he will stop barking if the defendant is not convicted—an allusion to Cleon's terrible voice [20] and an echo of *Knights* 1017-24, where Cleon speaks of himself as a dog who barks to protect the people.

The same opposition as in the domestic trial scene underlies the only remaining passage, outside the parabaseis, in which Cleon is mentioned, the passage in which Bdelycleon instructs his father in proper behavior at a dinner-party. The opposition does not emerge, however, from Bdelycleon's stated motives, which are consistently hedonistic and unrelated to social class. He only wants his father to enjoy life more. [21] Nor does it emerge from the first stages of the instruction—in how to dress (1122-73) and in how to carry on conversation with learned, clever men (1174-1207). Philocleon is utterly recalcitrant and maladroit, but not because Bdelycleon is imposing upper-class attitudes along with his practical advice. As events will show, Philocleon is simply constitutionally incapable of the refinement that his son hoped would bring him greater pleasure. The ideological opposition comes out only in the third and final—and only successful—stage of the instruction, when he learns how to cap skolia (1208-49). Bdelycleon imagines as Philocleon's drinking companions Cleon, Theorus, and their friends. The whale at the symposium—the incongruity of Cleon and his ilk at an upper-class symposium is the primary joke. [22] The rough-and-ready Philocleon, who has shown himself incapable of learning anything else about his new way of life, instinctively comes up with skolia that undercut those of the other

[17] For the names, see MacDowell 1971 on 836 and 895.
[18] Cf. the portrait in Pl. *La.*
[19] Laches had proposed the one-year truce in effect at the time of *V.* (Thuc. 4.118.11). He supported Nicias' peace effort in 421 B.C. (Thuc. 5.43.2).
[20] 929-30. Cf. Sommerstein 1981 on *Eq.* 137.
[21] 340-41, 503-506, 719-24, 1003-6, 1125.
[22] I agree with MacDowell's explanation *(a)* on 1220.

guests and expose one or another of them as a thief (1227), as duplici-
tous (1241-42), or as boastful (1248). The ludicrousness of the situation is compounded by Bdelycleon's evocation of Theorus' grasping
Cleon by the hand and singing an aristocratic skolion. [23]

In both parabaseis, there occurs an autobiographical passage concerning Aristophanes' relations with Cleon. Although these
two passages differ considerably from each another, they both end
with reference to the present comedy (1037 ἔτι καὶ νυνὶ ~ 1291 εἶτα
νῦν) and its relation to Cleon, and they can be shown to corroborate
the preceding analysis of the references to Cleon in *Wasps,* which has
shown that Cleon is linked to the jury system and thus to Aristophanes' criticism thereof. The imagery with which Cleon is described
in the main parabasis is consistent with the representation of Cleon in
the rest of *Wasps.* Elsewhere a dog, he is in the parabasis the super-
dog, Cerberus, the 'Jagged-Toothed One' (1031; cf. *Eq.* 1030; *Pax*
313), and the rays of his eyes are Κύννης 'of Kynna,' a prostitute
(1032), which puns on κυνός 'of a dog'. Elsewhere in the play, the
only named flatterer of Cleon is Theorus (though 419 implies others).
In the parabasis, Cleon/Cerberus has a hundred heads of flatterers
licking around his head (1032-33). [24] Cleon's voice, mocked elsewhere
in the play, [25] is here in the parabasis a 'death-dealing torrent' (1034;
cf. *Eq.* 137). In his opposition to this monster, Aristophanes compares
himself to Heracles—the comic poet is the hero who purifies the city of
monsters like Cleon. [26] The image returns in *Peace,* in the year following the performance of *Wasps,* and the lines are repeated with slight
variations (*V.* 1029-37 ~ *Pax* 751-60). [27] Since Cleon is now dead,
however, the past tenses of the verbs take on a new significance.

The hero and the monster—these are the images of Aristophanes and Cleon at the level of comic representation. Outside
comedy, there was also a conflict. Cleon prosecuted Aristophanes
after the performance of *Babylonians* in 426 B.C. (schol. *Ach.* 378).
That was not the end of the matter. The second parabasis of *Wasps*
refers to further conflict. Aristophanes distinguishes two phases in the
period between *Knights* and the present comedy.

---

[23] The second line, which is quoted by the scholiast, appears as Theognis 854, a
place which makes the ideological associations of the skolion clear.
[24] MacDowell suggests that two other monsters, the hundred-headed Hydra and
the snake-haired Typhoeus/Typhon (cf. *Eq.* 511) are combined with Cerberus. But
Cerberus had on his back the heads of all sorts of snakes (Apollod. 2.5.12) and
Pindar said that he had a hundred heads (schol. *Il.* 8.368). Aristophanes'
description may be pure Cerberus.
[25] 36, 596, 929-30, 1228, 1287.
[26] Cf. section 2, n. 8 above.
[27] How hard should the image be pressed? Heracles went into Hades, captured
Cerberus without the use of weapons, brought him to Eurystheus, and then restored
him to Hades (Apollod. 2.5.12).

(1) Cleon attacked me (1285-1286a), and, while I was under attack, others were only interested to know if I would retaliate with a joke (1286b-89). When I saw their reaction, I played a trick on them by pretending to be reconciled to Cleon (1290 and 1284) (and I thus seemed to deprive them of the joke they wanted, i.e. of a play like *Knights*; I gave them *Clouds*). (2) But now (1291), i.e. in *Wasps,* I have let Cleon down by returning to the offensive (and I have thus gratified the onlookers whom I at first disappointed with my feigned reconciliation with Cleon). With εἶτα νῦν 'and now' (1291), i.e. in *Wasps,* compare in the first parabasis ἔτι καὶ νυνί (1037) of Aristophanes' continued attack on Cleon. Each parabasis in *Wasps* concludes its section on Cleon with the poet's assertion that he has not abandoned the attack. [28] The second parabasis, with its complaint that the onlookers (1287 θεώμενοι) were only hoping for some Aristophanic retaliation against Cleon, continues the theme, typical of the parabasis, of the audience's injustice—'the poet now desires to blame the spectators' (1016). In the situation referred to in lines 1286b-89, the on-lookers, who are outside the affair (cf. schol. 1287), are, ironically, the would-be audience of the Aristophanic comedy they did not get. On this interpretation of 1284-91, Aristophanes is saying that he has in fact attacked Cleon, and he presupposes that the audience knew all along that 62-63 were indeed a *praeteritio* and that Cleon was under attack along with the jury system which he sponsored and by which his policies were supported.

Lines 1284-91 thus provide the autobiographical basis of the comic poet's function as purifier of the city, which is expressed in the image of Heracles in the first parabasis. As Heracles, he is relentless. As the comic poet-citizen, harassed by Cleon, he will never be reconciled with his enemy. Whereas the image of Heracles in the main parabasis might be interpreted as completely comic-poetic, the lines on Cleon in the second parabasis are inexplicable except as autobiography. They are pointless if the audience cannot connect them with events that have taken place in Athens before the performance of *Wasps.*

---

[28] The aorist in 1291 (ἐξηπάτηcεν) is to be expected in a proverb and can thus refer to the present, contrary to Halliwell 1980:35 n. 11.

10. The Politics of Aristophanes

The conclusions of sections 8 and 9 might seem to provide an implicit answer to the question of Aristophanes' politics that was alluded to at the beginning of this monograph. I believe that they do and that it would be appropriate at this point to take a stand on that question. In order to do so, however, one has to face a prior question and that is: granted that Aristophanes had political views and that they are expressed in his comedies, why should we think that they were seriously meant? One has also to distinguish between the historicity of Aristophanes' comedy and its seriousness. To take the notorious example of Socrates in *Clouds,* it may be, as Dover has argued, [1] that Aristophanes' Socrates-portrait is unhistorical; at the same time, Aristophanes could have intended serious criticism of Socrates. [2] Two kinds of arguments, however, have been used for a generally unserious, uncommitted attitude on Aristophanes' part.

One is the argument that, in the context of the festival, what comedy provided was not serious criticism of persons, policies or institutions but merely irreverent, satiric freedom of speech. [3] Putting aside the question whether the Lenaea and the City Dionysia (at which tragedies and dithyrambs were also performed) were festivals of the type assumed by this argument, one can observe that the comedies of Aristophanes provide strong evidence that the comic poet wished to speak about the affairs of the city, that he laid claim to a didactic function. The most important passage is the one in *Acharnians* in which Dicaeopolis, who has identified himself as Aristophanes (441), asserts that comedy ($\tau\rho\nu\gamma\omega\delta\iota\alpha$), too, knows what justice is (496-501). In this scene, Dicaeopolis is already playing the part of Telephus, the nobleman disguised as a beggar, for reasons that have to do with Aristophanes'-Dicaeopolis' peace policy. [4] In the same context, Aristophanes refers to Cleon's attack on him of the previous year (502-503). The reference must be taken as autobiographical, not simply because of the scholium to this effect on line 378, which mentions an indictment, but still more because of the style of these lines, which is quite straightforward. In fact, few have ever doubted that Aristophanes

---

[1] Dover 1968:xxxii-lvii.
[2] Forrest 1975:18 remarks: "from the fact that someone is not commenting seriously it does not follow that he is not commenting with serious intentions." Forrest's article addresses itself directly to Gomme 1938. See also Forrest 1986.
[3] Halliwell 1984a:7-9.
[4] Edmunds 1980:9-12.

was referring to a real enmity. [5] Just as in the second parabasis of *Wasps*, discussed in the preceding section, Aristophanes uses comedy as his means of retaliation against Cleon. Furthermore, the passage in *Acharnians* shows that Aristophanes uses a specifically comic technique, paratragedy, to this end. Comic style does not cancel out, it may bring out, serious concerns.

And in fact comedy was taken seriously. We know of two decrees that sought to blunt the effect of comedy. In the archonship of Morychides (440/39 B.C.) a decree forbade κωμῳδεῖν, i.e. ridicule; it was rescinded after three years in the archonship of Euthymenes (437/6 B.C.) (schol. Ar. *Ach.* 67). In about 415 B.C., a decree was passed μὴ κωμῳδεῖcθαι ὀνομαcτί τινα 'that no one be ridiculed by name'. [6] Even apart from such decrees, the comic poet was liable for what he said in his plays. Cleon's reaction to *Babylonians* has already been mentioned. [7] Because Aristophanes had criticized Athens' treatment of her allies at the Dionysia, when foreigners were present, Cleon hauled him before the Boulē (*Ach.* 377-82 and schol. on 378; cf. *Ach.* 502-503, 515-16, 659-64). [8] Aristophanes intimates in *Acharnians* that he will retaliate (300-302)—the lines seem to refer to the play of the following year, *Knights*. Cleon then took the further action against Aristophanes to which he refers in *Wasps* (1284-91).

Whether or not, then, Aristophanes meant seriously what he said in and through his comedies, he was taken seriously. *Clouds* is the clearest case. In Plato's *Apology of Socrates*, Socrates distinguishes between his present accusers, who have brought him to trial in 399 B.C. (24b2-27e), and his earlier accusers (18a7-24b2), whose charges correspond exactly to the main activities described in *Clouds* (18b7-8, 19b4-5). He does not know their names, 'unless one of them happens to be a comic poet' (18d1-2), whom he then names as Aristophanes (19c2), linking the charges to 'the comedy' (*ibid.*), i.e. *Clouds*. [9]

---

[5] To have shown, as Rosen 1983:ch. 4 has done, that there is a basis in archaic iambic poetry for the satire of Cleon in *Eq.* is not to have shown even *pro tanto* that Aristophanes' hatred of Cleon was fictional. (Was Thucydides'?)

[6] Schol. Ar. *Av.* 1297. On these decrees and the more problematical "Lex Antimachea," see A. Körte 1921:cols. 1234-35; Halliwell 1984b:86-87.

[7] Welsh 1978: "It is only necessary to cite the second performance of the *Frogs* and Cleon's reaction to the *Babylonians* to show that in Aristophanes' day it was accepted that Old Comedy *could* be a vehicle for the expression of serious (or even dangerous) views."

[8] Welsh 1978:108-75.

[9] Later in the *Apology*, in explaining why he never went into politics, he says, 'The reason is the one you have often heard from me in many places, that a certain god-like or divine thing *(theion ti kai daimonion)* comes to me, which thing Meletus [one of his accusers] ridiculed *(epikōmōdōn)* in the very indictment' (31c-d). In *epikōmōdōn* the preverb might mean 'after', 'in addition' so that the verb would mean 'ridiculing (my *daimonion*) after, in addition to the comedy [i.e. the *Clouds*] in which it had already been ridiculed'. (Examples of the preverb in these senses in Schwyzer, *GG* 2.465-466.) If so, the *daimonion* was ridiculed in *Nub.*, as I have argued in Edmunds 1985c.

In Xenophon's *Symposium,* of which the dramatic date is 421 B.C., two years after the production of *Clouds,* the Syracusan tells Socrates that he is known as τῶν μετεώρων φροντιστής (6.6), i.e. as the character represented in *Clouds,* [10] the Socrates who in 399 B.C. became the victim of Aristophanes' comic accusation (with the places in Xenophon and *Clouds* just cited cf. Pl. *Apol.* 18b7: μετέωρα φροντιστής). An Aristophanic comedy could be devastatingly funny. [11]

In passing, I want to stress the personal dimension of Aristophanes' conflict with Cleon, having concentrated on the political and the ideological. As a member of the same deme, Kydathēnaion, as Aristophanes, Cleon was in a position to cause difficulties for the young poet during his *dokimasia.* [12] Although most of the facts of the conflict sketched out above are irrecoverable, local animosities played a part. Hermann Lind has recently called attention to the cult table from Kydathēnaion. [13] The table, which belonged to a thiasos of Heracles, bears the members' names. The priest was Simon. In *Knights,* a Simon and a Panaitios are the only two Knights of the chorus who are named. If Simon was hipparch with Panaitios in 425/4 B.C. (schol. *Eq.* 243), he could be the same Simon who wrote a treatise on horsemanship (Xen. *de re eq.* 1.3; 11.6)—the first to do so according to Pliny (*NH* 34.76). [14] The probability is thus great that, as in the case of Amphitheos in *Acharnians* (46, 175), Aristophanes has made a fellow demesman a character in a comedy. [15] There is also the fact that another member of the thiasos, Philonides, was one of Aristophanes' chorodidaskaloi (hyp. ii *Av.,* hyp. i *Ran.,* schol. *Nub.* 531). Yet another member of the thiasos, Antitheos, may be the Amphitheos mentioned at *Thesmophoriazusae* 898. When, therefore, Aristophanes says that he will get vengeance on Cleon for the Knights (*Ach.* 300-302), personal loyalties and personal, deme-centered animosities are at work. When Aristophanes, in his opposition to Cleon, compares himself to a Heracles (section 9 above), the comic imposture has special meaning for the members of a thiasos in Kydathēnaion.

The other kind of argument against seriousness or committedness on Aristophanes' part maintains that Aristophanes is a poet and a dramatist and nothing else. Aristophanes' aims are strictly

---

[10] The word φροντιστής first appears in *Nub.* (266). In this play Socrates keeps a φροντιστήριον 'thinktank'.

[11] *Clouds* is also interesting in connection with the question of Aristophanes' seriousness in that it was revised after its failure in the dramatic competition of 423 B.C. and, although apparently never performed and in fact unperformable, was allowed to pass into circulation. See Dover 1968:xcviii, 270.

[12] Welsh 1978:138-51.

[13] IG II²2343. Lind 1985.

[14] The little treatise about the physique of horses which has come down under the name Simon does not seem to be the one Xenophon is referring to.

[15] Cf. Edmunds 1980:3-4. See Lind 1985:252 n.17 for the view that Amphitheos is not a real person.

artistic. [16] This position is contradicted by much that has already been said under the heading of seriousness. It seems to leave unexplained that constant feature of Old Comedy, rupture of dramatic illusion, [17] and to be unable to account for the parabasis. [18] Aristophanes' direct engagement with the audience has, of course, its own artistry, but this cannot be an artistry for its own sake or simply for the sake of laughs. By drawing attention to itself as poetry, Aristophanic comedy ultimately puts its many topical allusions and impersonations of contemporary persons in an ambiguous position. On the one hand, they have the status of laughable comic inventions, and Aristophanes is free of blame, no matter what he alleges; on the other, they are clearly distinguishable from the medium in which they appear. Therefore what is most poetic can be most real, and when Aristophanes is most comical he can be most serious.

This principle can also be found at work in the general plan of an Aristophanic comedy, and can be illustrated from a play, *Thesmophoriazusae*, which would seem an unpromising basis for the observations set forth in the preceding paragraph. Unlike the other surviving examples of Old Comedy, it has a single plot-line, carried through from beginning to end, with a consistent parody of tragedy which is apparently the play's main concern. Nevertheless, it has serious political concerns. The following diagram represents the relation of the play to the context of performance:

---

[16] Gomme 1938:97-109 is the canonical statement. Halliwell 1984a has continued this line of thought.
[17] Sifakis 1971:7-14.
[18] The difficulties of understanding the parabasis on the basis of modern assumptions concerning drama underlie the discussion of Pickard-Cambridge 1962:197-199. For bibliography, see Bowie:1982:27-40, who argues that the parabasis "has a significant role as the focus of the most important themes in the play" (p. 27).

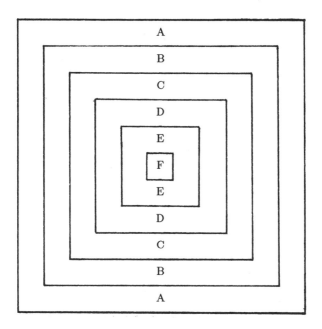

The outermost square (A) represents Athens. Within Athens, there is the dramatic festival (B)—in the case of *Thesmophoriazusae* it was probably the Dionysia. At this festival, *Thesmophoriazusae* (C) is performed. The setting of the comedy is Athens (D). In this setting, a festival, the Thesmophoria, is being celebrated (E). At this festival, an ekklēsia is held (F). The business of the ekklēsia, namely, the prosecution of Euripides (81-84, 181-82, 378-79) provides the occasion for the intrigue that forms the plot of *Thesmophoriazusae.*

The diagram shows that the setting of the play (D-F) approximately replicates the context (A-C) of performance: the pattern in each case is city-festival-production, where "production" means in the one case a dramatic production, i.e. of *Thesmophoriazusae,* and in the other an ekklēsia, which is the occasion for the reproduction of various scenes from Euripidean tragedy. The anomalous thing in this pattern, which calls attention to itself as an anomaly, is the women's ekklēsia. [19] In this way, the city of the setting (D), corresponding to the real Athens (A), reappears within the festival (E), and Athens (A) is thus represented at the center of the play in the women's ekklēsia. The link between the two Athenses (A and F) is established by the parody, which is far longer than the plot requires, [20]

---

[19] Both because of the very idea of women holding an ekklēsia and also because, in general, a meeting of the ekklēsia would not be held on a festival day. See Mikalson 1975:1-7, 182-197.
[20] Wilamowitz 1893:348.

of the opening ceremony of the Athenian ekklēsia (295-379). This ceremony begins with the bidding prayer of the *kerykaina* (295-311). This long passage of prose, the longest in any of Aristophanes' comedies, has in its very sound and rhythm the effect of pointing outside the setting, outside the Thesmophoria, to the real ekklēsia that is being parodied. This effect is guaranteed by the close imitation of the procedure and language of official ritual. [21]

The concern, then, is Athens itself and in particular the safety of the democratic constitution. There is general agreement that the references to tyranny and 'bringing back the tyrant' (338-39, 1143-46) are references to Alcibiades, [22] and in the second of these passages the reappearance of the δῆμος γυναικῶν is notable. [23] The references in the parabasis to base trierarchs and bad steersmen and to Hyperbolus (836-45) point to Samos, where Hyperbolus was at the time [24] and where the oligarchic movement had already begun (Thuc. 8.47-48.1). But the internal threat is paramount. In the parabasis, the chorus institutes an invidious comparison between men and women based on the contrast between typical women's names and particular Athenian men or particular male civic functions. In lines 808-809, they say:

ἀλλ' Εὐβούλης τῶν πέρυσίν τις βουλευτής ἐστιν ἀμείνων
παραδοὺς ἑτέρῳ τὴν βουλείαν; οὐδ' αὐτὸς τοῦτο φήσει.

But is there any of last year's senators better than Euboulē [She of Good Counsel], since he has given his office to another? Not even he himself will say so. [25]

If, as is now widely believed, *Thesmophoriazusae* was produced in 411, [26] the reference is to the process by which, beginning in 413 B.C., some of the Boulē's powers were handed over to the board of probouloi. [27] The force of the reference comes from the dramatic situation. The chorus in this parabasis retains its dramatic character. It is a chorus of women holding an ekklēsia. At the Thesmophoria, they thus put

----

[21] Haldane 1965:39-46. Fraenkel 1961:131-35 compares Aesch. *Sept.* 182-86 with this passage in *Th.*
[22] On the metrical emphasis given the reference to tyranny in the second of these passages, see Wilamowitz 1921:592; Dale 1968:166; *HCT* 5:193.
[23] *HCT ibid.*
[24] Probably; he was there later anyway: Thuc. 8.73 puts his murder at the hands of the oligarchs at the time of the revolution of the 400, i.e. June 411 B.C.
[25] Reading Kuster's φήcει for ms. φήcειc.
[26] Sommerstein, 1977:112-26 and Andrewes, *HCT* 5:184-93, approaching the matter quite differently, have both reached this conclusion. Jeffrey Henderson, in the introduction to his edition of *Lys.* forthcoming in the Oxford series, provides a thorough discussion of the events of 411 B.C. in relation to internal evidence in *Lys.* and concludes that the play was produced at the Lenaea.
[27] *HCT* 5:188.

into effect the institutions of the Cleisthenian constitution. They can send to the prytaneis (763-64), one of whom arrives (929ff.) to carry out the resolution of the Boulē (943-44). In the women's Athens, the Boulē is still effective; it is the men who are destroying the constitution in the real Athens, which is thus brought into the play.

Aristophanes has designed *Thesmophoriazusae* in such a way that at its very center, in the women's ekklēsia, a concern for Athens, a concern that cannot be other than serious, is expressed. At the same time, the plot of the comedy, which is built on the enmity between Euripides and the women of Athens, follows its own madcap course. The relation between this plot and the structure that has been diagrammed and analyzed is a subject that lies outside this discussion, which has been addressed to the question of the seriousness of Aristophanes' political views. [28] That question had to be discussed before the question, to which I now turn, of what those views were.

I begin with a quotation from G. E. M. de Ste. Croix' essay, "The political outlook of Aristophanes": [29]

> It seems to me that Aristophanes was a man of very vigorous political views of a conservative, 'Cimonian' variety (not at all untypical among the Athenian upper classes), the general complexion of which is easily identifiable from the plays and remained consistent over the period of some forty years during which he was writing comedies. . . .Why anyone should suppose that they were not meant seriously, or were not intended to influence the audience, I cannot imagine.

With the point concerning Aristophanes' seriousness, everything that has been said in this paper concurs. As for de Ste. Croix' description of Aristophanes' views, the present readings of *Knights* and of *Thesmophoriazusae* do not support it. De Ste. Croix combines *Knights* and the parabasis of *Frogs* as expressions of the same political outlook, but *Knights* is saying something quite different from that parabasis. The Knights themselves have nihilistically invited the Sausage-seller to show that their own values are meaningless, and Aristophanes, in order to make the intended defeat of Cleon acceptable, is willing to sacrifice the Knights along with their values. It is worth remembering that the Knights are *not* called *kaloi te kagathoi* in *Knights*, and thus they cannot be equated with the *kaloi te kagathoi* of *Frogs*. The "great divide" of which de Ste. Croix speaks is not present in *Knights;* [30] Aristophanes has done everything to bridge it.

---

[28] See Zeitlin 1982:169-217.
[29] This essay appears as Appendix XXIX in de Ste. Croix 1972.
[30] De Ste. Croix 1972:374.

Furthermore, the final scene of *Knights* presents an Athens remarkably like that of the Periclean Funeral Oration in Thucydides. It is an imperial city in which the citizens enjoy the exercise of power and the pursuit of pleasure. This image of Athens suited Aristophanes' aims at the time of *Knights*. When, however, he refers to Pericles, it is only to make fun of him. [31]

Consistency of outlook is lacking not only over forty years but from play to play. If *Thesmophoriazusae* was produced at the Dionysia in 411 B.C., and if de Ste. Croix is right, then one would expect some sort of accomodation to the oligarchs. Aristophanes might, for example, have done as he did in *Knights* and suggested reconciliation. On the contrary, there is nothing in *Thesmophoriazusae* that does not reflect the point of view of the demos. [32] Although Aristophanes certainly held serious views and these can to some extent be established for individual plays, he cannot be pinned down to a consistent political outlook on the many, varied political issues of his lifetime. The reasons for the impossibility of so pinning him down undoubtedly have to do with the nature of Athenian political life, which, as is well known, was not organized in political parties and differed fundamentally from what we think of as politics. [33] On the other hand, it seems to me that it should be possible to define something like a consistent political ideal, as distinguished from a consistent view on matters of policy. This ideal, which may be specific to comic poetry, is that of the city at peace, the happy city, in which privacy, farming, devotion to the family, and piety, especially in the form of public feasting and festivals, are the way of life. One of the main ways this ideal, to which Cleon was clearly a major threat, emerges is from the various counter-Athenses that Aristophanes loved to create. There is the private peace of Dicaeopolis, who impersonates in name and in deed a polis and who in himself is a counter-Athens. There is Cloudcuckcooland, founded in explicit opposition to Athens. There are the female counter-Athenses of *Lysistrata* and *Ecclesiazusae*. But these are the fictions of comic poetry. The answers they provide to political questions seem to be more ideal than practical.

---

[31] *Ach.* 530-34; *Pax* 605-18. On the latter passage, see de Ste. Croix 1972:371 and n. 24.

[32] *HCT* 5:188, 192.

[33] Marxist analysis has contributed to elucidating the differences. Even if Aristophanes were an oligarch in de Ste. Croix' sense, the fact remains "che neppure nei sogni di restaurazione oligarchica compare mai l'accenno sia pur lontano a un'organizzazione statale che sia garante del mantenimento della stratificazione sociale. Lo stato in quanto autonomo apparato di gestione del potere, resta dimensione estranea alla tradizione aristocratica non meno che alla politicità democratica" (Lanza 1977:177).

Appendix

These are notes and comments on *Knights* that have appeared since the time of Dover 1957:76-79. Including those from Sommerstein 1980, they are usually either more detailed or more general than those in Sommerstein 1981. (Review by Edmunds 1985b.) Landfester 1967 is a fairly detailed commentary, and his views, like Sommerstein's, should be compared with those printed here. Kraus 1985 comments on many particulars; some, not all, of his observations are recorded below. Comments in square brackets are by L.E. [1]

2   The combination κακὸc κακῶc is "vigorous, colloquial Attic." Renehan 1976:114.

6ff.   The identification by Hypothesis II of one of the slaves as Nicias has no authority. Dover 1967:164-67. Also Dover 1959:196-99. The two slaves are Nicias and Demosthenes. Kraus 1985:115-19. [Cf. 89]

8-9   The construction: periphrasis consisting of verb plus object is equivalent to a transitive verb and governs a (second) object. This construction is common in tragedy. Renehan 1976:53.

54-55   Pun on Πύλοc and πύελοc. Cf. 1060 and 1172 Πυλαιμάχοc. Renehan 1976:100. Kraus 1985:115 n. 13.

63   τέχνην πεποίηται. Kraus 1985:195 calls attention to Burkert's discussion of a similar phrase in the Derveni papyrus in *ZPE* 47 (1982), Anhang, p. 9.

89   This line, taken in the context of the second slave's aversion to wine, suggests that the second slave represents Nicias, who was known for avoiding symposia (Plut. *Nic.* 5). Sommerstein 1980:46-47. Kraus

---

[1] I am grateful to Robert Renehan for suggestions on an earlier draft of this Appendix.

1985:124. [Cf. 6ff.]

92-93   Dionysus, or wine, is typically the source of real, or imagined, wealth. Slater 1976:165.

125-134   Eucrates (the hemp seller) and Lysicles (the sheep seller) "were followers of Pericles even though Aristophanes places them on a plane with Cleon." Kagan 1974:126-27.

167   Read λαικάσει (fut. mid.). The verb is synonymous with *irrumari / fellare*. Jocelyn 1980.

175   Read γ' for δ'. Fraenkel 1962:47-48.

190   Read τουτί σε μόνον ἔβλαψεν. Fraenkel 1962:45-46.

230-33   Cleon does not have a portrait-mask because there was nothing distinctive about his face. He simply has a hideous mask. The mask-maker is afraid not of retribution but of the very hideousness. Dover 1967:164-67. Cf. Chapman 1983:16. But Cratinus frag. 217A Edmonds shows that Cleon had especially ugly eyebrows. Welsh 1979:214-15. Kraus 1985:117 n. 16.

242-77   With *Pax* 296-45 and *Pl.* 253-321 these lines form a type of parodos: the chorus appears in order to aid an actor. Zimmermann 1984:30-31. The chorus' trochees express aggressiveness; and other stylistic features of the passage give it a militant character. Zimmermann 1984:57.

259-63   "There is constant play between the bribing of auditors. . . and crude sexual foreplay before violent rape." Nine words are singled out as having sexual connotations. Maxwell-Stewart 1972:43-44.

281   εἶτα (κᾆτα) and ἔπειτα (κἄπειτα), in various combinations of participle followed by finite verb, are especially characteristic of comic diction." Renehan 1976:147-48.

303/304   Read, with Coulon and Sommerstein, Dobree's καὶ κρᾶκτα τοῦ. Zimmermann 1985:119.

327   The reference here and at 794 is to Archeptolemos, son of Hippodamos of Miletus. Sommerstein 1980:47-48.

343   καρυκκοποιεῖν means 'to agitate', 'to stir up' (see Hesychius s.v. καρυκάςειν and καρυκείαις). Sommerstein 1980:49.

386   For ὧδ' of the codd. read οὗ (Sommerstein's conjecture) and assume a hiatus at the end of the line. Zimmermann 1985:119.

395   ςῇ is *Alltagssprache*. Fraenkel 1962:48-49.

407   Oulios the 'wheat-snooper', i.e. sitophylax, is freed of the threat of prosecution by Cleon. Sommerstein 1980:49-50.

438   Aristophanes "seems to implicate Cleon" in the bringing to trial of the generals who accepted the surrender of Potidaea (cf. Thuc. 2.70.4). Kagan 1974:98.

465   "Cleon appears to have tried even to bring Argos over to the Athenian camp. . . ." Kagan 1974:252 and 334. [Cf. on 811-19 below.]

495-97   Spoken by the first slave. Kraus 1985:116.

512-16   If there was a law prescribing a minimum age for requesting a chorus from the archon, it was not this which prevented Aristophanes from applying for his own chorus in 427-425 B.C. Halliwell 1980:33-34. [Cf. on 541-44.]

526-36   The metaphor in 532-33 is ambivalent. The vehicle [for this term see section 2 above] is both a couch and a lyre. This is the only such metaphor in Aristophanes. In the portrait of Cratinus, there is parody as well as praise. Perusino 1982.

541-44   "The progression to full κωμῳδοδιδασκαλία involved a number of stages, and this᾽is the reason why . . . Aristophanes chooses to use a metaphor that suggests a complex development. Part of the apprenticeship entailed contributing to the plays of others—a collaboration which may have been an established way of encouraging new dramatists, and which is not to be thought of as purely literary but rather as experience in the creation of a dramatic script for production." Halliwell 1980:43. [I have been unable to find Mastromarco 1979.] These lines refer to only two stages in the career of Aristophanes: 427-425 B.C., when Aristophanes did not produce his own plays, and 424 B.C. and after, when he did. Perusino 1980-81. Also MacDowell 1982, who makes the further point that the "secret" and "open" period referred to in *Vesp.* 1016-22 are these two stages. [The articles of Perusino and MacDowell, written independently of each other, are complementary, as are the articles of Halliwell and Mastromarco to which they reply.]

580   "It is evident from Ar. *Knights* 580 (supported by an almost certain emendation in Lys. xvi 18) that long hair characterized young men of the wealthiest class, and, in consequence, *komān,* 'wear the hair long' is used in comedy in the sense 'give oneself airs', 'think oneself a cut above other people' (e.g. *Wasps* 1317)." Dover 1978:78-79.

579-80   A contemporary phrase or slogan expressing opposition to the war. Boegehold 1982.

595-610   Ironic-serious praise of the horses replaces praise of the Knights. The horses are more ardent than the generals (cf. 602-604 with 576). "Le lien [between horses and Knights] est constamment souligné; non seulement les chevaux sont loués comme le sont dans un *épitaphios* les guerriers morts (v. 596: ἄξιοι δ᾽ εἷς᾽ εὐλογεῖσθαι), mais encore ils sont constamment comparés à leurs maîtres (v. 597: μεθ᾽ ἡμῶν; v. 599: ἀνδρικῶς; v. 601: ὥσπερ ἡμεῖς οἱ βροτοί) si bien qu'en 610, ἱππέας se substitue tout naturellement à ἵππους." Loraux 1981:312 n. 285.

608-10   "In view of the connexion with the Knights, doubts about Theorus' identity are unnecessary: this must be the associate of Cleon familiar from *Wasps* 42-51, 418 and 1236-41. But what is the point of the crab? The answer, I think, is that Aristophanes is here parodying not one but two skolia. One of the songs involved is obvious: Timocreon's skolion (*PMG* 731) had already been parodied in Dicaeopolis' version of the Megarian decree at *Acharnians* 533f. (cf. the similar riddle at *Wasps* 22f.). The other skolion is preserved in the collection of Athenaeus XV 694c ff. (=*PMG* 892; see Reitzenstein, *Epigramm und Skolion* [1893], pp. 19f.). The relevant detail of it is that it contains the utterance of a crab ὁ δὲ καρκίνος ὧδε ἔφα κτλ. There are few enough circumstances in which one might want to talk about the saying of a crab, even in comedy; the clearest context is a skolion or fable of the type cited. At *Knights* 608-10, then, Aristophanes is putting a mock skolion, compounded out of two existing skolia, into Theorus' mouth, as a witty way of portraying his annoyance at the recent Corinthian success of his and Cleon's enemies, the Knights. The comic technique may seem to us bizarre, but it is certainly Aristophanic, for it is employed at *Wasps* 1219ff." Halliwell 1982:153. [I have quoted the entire note on *Knights* because many will have difficulty in consulting the journal in which it appeared.] The Aesopic tale of the crab and the snake, which provides the context for the second of the skolia cited by Halliwell, occurs in a fuller form in a modern Greek folktale. Megas 1970:20, 217-18.

639   *Katapūgōn* connotes a passive homosexual role. Dover 1978:142. West 1977:27f. is cited for alteration of the anus by habitual buggery.

656   Does not provide an example of θύω with double accusative, as LSJ s.v. θύω (A) I.5 state, citing this passage. εὐαγγελία (sc. ἱερά) is in apposition with βοῦς: "sacrifice a hundred oxen *as* thank-offerings for the good news." Renehan 1969:123.

730-33   Perhaps allusion to Sappho frag. 1. Renehan 1976:87-88, who observed that τίς ἀδικεῖ σε was doubtless commonplace. [He now compares Eur. *Bacch.* 320-21.]

736-40   Reflects "generalised hostility to boys who play the role of eromenoi." Dover 1978:146.

763-823   The epirrhema is in anapests because it begins with a prayer to Athena. Zimmermann 1985:118. [Cf. 843-910.]

786   Cleon may have been connected by marriage with the house of Harmodius. Perhaps "Demos now expects that anyone else aspiring to be his benefactor will lay claim to a similar connection?" Sommerstein 1980:50. Contra: Bourriot 1982.

794   [See on 327.]

797   "Aristophanes puts in the mouth of the Paphlagonian slave who represents Cleon in the *Knights* the determination to let the Athenian demos rule over all the Greeks, but, as usual, it is hard to know if this is meant to reproduce a position really taken by Cleon or is mere comic exaggeration." Kagan 1974:238.

814   Cf. Plut. *Them.* 31.1. Aristophanes refers to Themistocles' activities as controller of water-supplies. Sommerstein 1980:50-51.

811-19   "Both [Cleon and Pericles] thought that a lasting peace could only be won if Sparta was broken or completely humiliated. This had been Themistocles' view and it is interesting that in this year [424 B.C.] Cleon boasted his rivalry with Themistocles. He may partly have been thinking of his [Themistocles'] attempts to win over neutral Argos." Meiggs 1972:319. In n. 2 on this page, Meiggs draws attention to the possible significance of the reference to Argos in 813. [Cf. Neil 1901 on 813 who, like Meiggs in n. 3 on the same page, refers to *Eq.* 465, where the Sausage-seller accuses Cleon of dealings with the Argives. Note also that 813 *init.* is paratragic—an example of the poet's expression of a political view through a specifically comic device.] Meiggs continues: "Like Themistocles before him and Alcibiades after him Cleon perhaps realised that the most effective way to fight Sparta was in the Peloponnese with her discontented allies. This policy depended on an alliance with Argos."

843-910   The antepirrhema is in iambs, which show the bold-
           ness of Cleon/Paphlagon. Zimmermann 1985:118.
           [Cf. 763-823.]

847   Punctuate after the first word in the line. Fraenkel
           1962:49-50.

877-80   Cleon apparently refers to a successful prosecution
           like Aiskhines' of Timarkhos. The Sausage-seller's
           retort shows how the "man in the street consoles
           himself with the thought that those who run his life
           politically and order him about are in fact his inferi-
           ors, no better than prostitutes, homosexually subordi-
           nate." Dover 1978:141-42.

1036-44   Through the unmistakable allusion at 1037 to Hero-
           dotus 6.131.2, Paphlagon/Cleon claims to be a second
           Pericles—a claim that Aristophanes found intolerable.
           Euripides may have taken his cue from Aristophanes
           in turning Theseus in *Suppl.* "into a political hero
           and a dramatic prototype of Pericles." The similarity
           of *Suppl.* 352 to *Eq.* 1330 supports this notion.
           Podlecki 1975-6:25-26.

1042-44   With Arist. *Pol.* 1316a29 and Alcaeus 296(P2)a8
           (Antileon was worthy to be flayed ἀπυδέρθην) cf. Sol.
           frag. 33 W ('if I could be tyrant of Athens for one day
           I would be willing to be flayed') and these lines
           (1042-44) in *Eq.* "If the Antileon whom Demos has in
           mind is none other than the tyrant of Chalcis, the
           joke is not without point." Lloyd-Jones 1975. [Curi-
           ously the phrase ἀсκὸс. . .δεδάρθαι (cf. Sol. frag. 33.7
           W) occurs at *Eq.* 370.]

1103   ". . .I would suggest that the use of the term
           ὑπογραμματεύс for Thouphanes in Σ^{Vr} *Kn.* 1103 is
           an extension of the interpretation of *Kn.* 1256 found
           in Σ^{VE} on this later passage." Halliwell 1984b:86.

1111-50   A special form of the encomiastic *amoibaion*. In the
           dramatic action, it prepares for the epiphany of the
           final scene. Zimmermann 1984:200-03.

1150   The acc. should give not the probing instrument but the cavity to be probed. κημόν is a surprise substitute for e.g. λαιμόν. 'Probing the funnel' refers to the act of voting. Sommerstein 1980:51.

1225   The schol. on this line refers not to the Helots but to a play called *Helots*. This line should be included in the fragments of Eupolis' comedy by that name. The reference in Eupolis frag. 78 to plagiarism by Aristophanes is to this line. (Frag. 78 ends with the same word as line 1225.) Eupolis is replying with *tu quoque* to Aristophanes' charge against him in *Clouds* 553-4. Sommerstein 1980:51-53.

1242   The verb is passive. Dover 1978:141 and n. 8. [Cf. 428].

1245-47   Shows "commercial activity going on elsewhere than in the Agora." de Ste. Croix 1972:268-69.

1249   Deardon 1976:70-71 is right that Paphlagon is removed by means of the *ekkyklema* but wrong that it was brought out after 751. It was brought out as 1250-52 were spoken. Sommerstein 1980:53-54.

1264-1315   The second parabasis, following the final defeat of Paphlagon/Cleon and marking the end of the main action, provides a pause before the surprising turn of events in the final scene. Zimmermann 1985:175-76.

1300-04   Hyperbolus did not in fact make such a proposal. de Ste. Croix 1972:222-23. On de Ste. Croix's methodological principles here: Chapman 1978:60.

1326-34   The 'Athens of Old' is represented by a symbolic building rolled out on the *ekkyklema*. Sommerstein 1980:54-56.

1330   [See on 1036-44.]

1399   [Spyropoulos 1981 was unavailable in the eleven libraries in the U.S. in which I tried to find it.]

Bibliography

Adam, James 1920. *The Republic of Plato,* vol. 1. Cambridge.

Adkins, A. W. H. 1976. "POLUPRAGMOSUNE and 'Minding One's Own Business': A Study in Greek Social and Political Values." *CP* 71:301-27.

Albini, U. 1965. "Osservazioni sui Cavalieri di Aristofane." *Maia* 17:3-18.

Alföldi A. 1967. "Die Herrschaft der Reiterei in Griechenland und Rom nach dem Sturz der Könige." In *Gestalt und Geschichte: Festschrift Karl Schefold zu seinem sechigsten Geburtstag am 26. Januar 1965,* edd. Martha Rohde-Liegle, Herbert A. Cahn, and H. Chr. Ackermann, pp. 13-47. Francke Verlag. Bern.

Allinson, F. G. 1880. "On πῖαρ as an Adjective." *AJP* 1:458.

Allison, J. W. 1979. "Thucydides and ΠΟΛΥΠΡΑΓΜΟΣΥΝΗ." *AJAH* 4:10-22.

⸺⸺⸺ 1979b. "Additional Note." *AJAH* 4:157-58.

Alty, J. 1982. "Dorians and Ionians." *JHS* 102:1-14.

ATL Merritt, B. D., H. T. Wade-Gery, and M. F. McGregor, 1939-53. *The Athenian Tribute Lists.* 4 vols. Cambridge, MA.

Barron, John P. 1964. "Religious Propaganda of the Delian League." *JHS* 84:35-48.

Bechtel, Friederich 1914. *Lexilogus zu Homer.* Halle.

Benveniste, Emile 1969. *Le vocabulaire des institutions indo-européennes,* vol. 1. Les Editions de Minuit. Paris.

Boegehold, Alan L. 1982. "A Dissent at Athens ca 424-421 B.C." *GRBS* 23:147-56.

Boersma, Joh. S. 1970. *Athenian Building Policy from 561/0 to 405/4 B.C.* Scripta Archaeologica Groningana 4. Wolters-Noordhoff Publishing. Groningen.

Bourriot, F. 1982. "La Famille et le milieu sociale de Cléon." *Historia* 31:418-30.

Bowie, A. M. 1982. "The Parabasis in Aristophanes: Prolegomena, *Acharnians.*" *CQ* 32:27-40.

75

Bowra, Sir Maurice 1961. *Greek Lyric Poetry*, 2nd ed. Clarendon Press. Oxford.

—————— 1969. *The Odes of Pindar*. Penguin Books. Harmondsworth, UK.

Bugh, Glenn R. 1979. "The Athenian Cavalry from the Sixth to the Fourth Century B.C." Ph.D. diss., University of Maryland.

Burton, R. W. B. 1962. *Pindar's Pythian Odes*. Oxford University Press. London.

Butler, Christopher 1984. *Interpretation, Deconstruction and Ideology*. Clarendon Press. Oxford.

Campbell, D. A. 1986. "Ship Imagery in the *Oedipus Tyrannus*. In M. Cropp, E. Fantham, and S. E. Scully, edd. *Greek Tragedy and its Legacy, essays presented to D. J. Conacher*, pp. 115-20. The University of Calgary Press. Calgary.

Carne-Ross, D. S. 1985. *Pindar*. Yale University Press. New Haven and London.

Cassio, A. C. 1985. *Commedia e partecipazione: La "Pace" di Aristofane*. Forme materiali e ideologie del mondo antico 14. Liguori. Naples.

Cerri, G. 1969. " Ἴcoc δαcμόc come equivalente di ἰcovoμία nella silloge teognidea." *QUCC* 8:97-104.

Chapman, G. A. H. 1978. "Aristophanes and History." *Acta Classica* 21:59-70.

—————— 1983. "Dramatic Illusion in Aristophanes." *AJP* 104:1-23.

Clay, Diskin 1972. "Epicurus' Kυρία Δόξα XVII." *GRBS* 13:59-66.

Connor, W. R. 1971. *The New Politicians of Fifth-Century Athens*. Princeton University Press. Princeton.

Cook, A. B. 1940. *Zeus*, vol. 3. Cambridge University Press. Cambridge.

Cranston, Maurice 1975. "Ideology." In *The New Encyclopaedia Britannica, Macropaedia*, vol. 9, pp. 194-98.

Culham, Phyllis 1978. "The Delean League: Bicameral or Unicameral?" *AJAH* 3: 29-30.

Dale, A. M. 1968. *The Lyric Metres of Greek Drama*, 2nd ed. Cambridge University Press. Cambridge.

Deardon, C. W. 1976. *The Stage of Aristophanes*. London.

Derrida, Jacques 1981. *Dissemination*. Trans. Barbara Johnson. The University of Chicago Press. Chicago.

Detienne, M. 1973. *Les maîtres de vérite' dans la grèce archaïque*, 2nd ed. Maspero. Paris.

Dickie, M. W. 1984. "Hesychia and Hybris in Pindar." In *Greek Poetry and Philosophy: Studies in Honor of Leonard Woodbury*, ed. D.E. Gerber, pp. 83-109. Scholar's Press. Chico, CA.

Dienelt, K. 1953. "Apragmosyne." *WS* 66:94-104.

Donlan, W. 1970. "Changes and Shifts in the Meaning of Demos in the Literature of the Archaic Period." *PP* 135:381-95.

_____ 1980. *The Aristocratic Ideal in Ancient Greece: Attitudes of Superiority from Homer to the End of the Fifth Century B.C.* Coronado Press. Lawrence, KS.

Dover, K. J. 1957. "Aristophanes 1938-1955." *Lustrum* 2:52-112.

_____ 1959. "Aristophanes, Knights 11-20." *CR* 73 = NS 9:196-99.

_____ 1968. *Aristophanes: Clouds.* Clarendon Press. Oxford.

_____ 1972. *Aristophanic Comedy.* University of California Press. Berkeley and Los Angeles.

_____ 1975. "Portrait-Masks in Aristophanes." In *Aristophanes und die alte Komödie*, ed. H. J. Newiger, pp. 155-73. Wege der Forschung, vol. 265. Darmstadt. = ΚΩΜΩΙΔΟΤΡΑΓΗΜΑΤΑ: *Studia Aristophanea viri Aristophanei W J W Koster in honorem*, pp. 16-28. Amsterdam.

_____ 1978. *Greek Homosexuality.* Cambridge, MA.

Edmunds, Lowell 1975. "Thucydides' Ethics as Reflected in the Description of Stasis (3.82-83)." *HSCP* 79:73-92.

_____ 1980. "Aristophanes' 'Acharnians'." In *Aristophanes: Essays in Interpretation*, ed. Jeffrey Henderson. *YCS* 26:1-41.

_____ 1985a. "The Genre of Theognidean Poetry," in *Theognis of Megara*, edd. G. Nagy and T. Figueira, pp. 96-111. Johns Hopkins University Press. Baltimore and London.

_____ 1985b. Review of Sommerstein 1981. In *AJP* 106:381-83.

_____ 1985c. "Aristophanes' Socrates." In Proceedings of the Boston Area Colloquium in Ancient Philosophy, vol. 1, ed. J. J. Cleary, pp. 209-40.

Ehrenberg, V. 1935. *Ost und West: Studien zur geschichtlichen Problematik der*

Antike. Rohrer. Brünn.

_____ 1947. "Polypragmosyne: A Study in Greek Politics." *JHS* 67:44-67 = *Polis and Imperium* (Zurich 1965), pp. 466-501.

_____ 1951. *The People of Aristophanes.* Basil Blackwell. Oxford.

Farnell, L. R. 1932. *The Works of Pindar.* Macmillan. London.

Fennell, C. A. M. 1893. *Pindar: The Olympian and Pythian Odes.* Cambridge University Press. Cambridge.

Figueira, Thomas 1985. "The Theognidea and Megarian Society." In *Theognis of Megara*, edd. G. Nagy and T. Figueira, pp. 112-58. Johns Hopkins University Press. Baltimore and London.

Fornara, C. W. 1970. "The Cult of Harmodius and Aristogeiton." *Philologus* 114:171-80.

_____ 1973. "Cleon's Attack Against the Cavalry." *CQ* NS 23:24.

Forrest, W. G. 1975. "Aristophanes and the Athenian Empire." In B.M. Levick, ed. *The Ancient Historian and his Materials. Essays in Honor of C.E. Stevens on his seventieth birthday*, pp. 17-29. Trowbridge and Esher. Farnborough, Hants.

_____ 1986. "The Stage and Politics." In M. Cropp, E. Fantham, and S. E. Scully, edd. *Greek Tragedy and its Legacy, essays presented to D. J. Conacher*, pp. 229-39. The University of Calgary Press. Calgary.

Fraenkel, Eduard 1961. "Aeschylea." *MH* 18:131-135.

_____ 1962. *Beobachtungen zu Aristophanes.* Rome.

Frisk, H. 1960. *Griechisches etymologisches Wörterbuch.* Carl Winter. Heidelberg.

Gelzer, T. 1960. *Der epirrhematische Agon bei Aristophanes: Untersuchungen zur Struktur der attischen alten Komödie.* Zetemata 23. Munich.

Gentili, Bruno 1984. *Poesia e pubblico nella grecia antica da Omero al V secolo.* Laterza. Rome.

Giannini, P. 1982. "'Qualcuno' e 'nessuno' in Pind. *Pyth.* 8,95." *QUCC* 40 = NS 11:69-76.

Gildersleeve, B. L. 1899. *Pindar: The Olympian and Pythian Odes.* Harper & Brothers. New York. Repr. Arno Press Inc. 1979.

Gomme, A. W. 1938. "Aristophanes and Politics." *CR* 52:97-109 = *More Essays in*

Greek History and Literature (Oxford, 1962), pp. 70-91.

Graham, A. J. 1983. *Colony and Mother City in Ancient Greece,* 2nd ed. Ares Publishers, Inc. Chicago.

Greenhalgh, P. A. L. 1973. *Early Greek Warfare: Horsemen and Chariots in the Homeric and Archaic Ages.* Cambridge University Press. Cambridge.

Griffith, M. 1983. Ed., *Aeschylus: Prometheus Bound.* Cambridge University Press. Cambridge.

Grossmann, G. 1950. *Politische Schlagwörter aus der Zeit des Peloponnesischen Krieges.* Leemann. Zurich. Repr. Arno Press Inc. 1973.

HCT Gomme, A. W., A. Andrewes and K. J. Dover 1945-1981. *A Historical Commentary on Thucydides.* 5 vols. Oxford.

Händel, P. 1963. *Formen und Darstellungsweisen in der aristophanischen Komödie.* Heidelberg.

Haldane, J. A. 1965. "A Scene in the *Thesmophoriazusae* (295-371)." *Philologus* 109:39-46.

Halliwell, Stephen 1980. "Aristophanes' Apprenticeship." *CQ* NS 30:33-45.

─────── 1982. "Notes on some Aristophanic jokes (*Ach.* 854-9; *Kn.* 608-10; *Peace* 695-9; *Thesm.* 605; *Frogs* 1039)." *LCM* 7:153-54.

─────── 1984a. "Aristophanic Satire." *The Yearbook of English Studies* 14:6-20.

─────── 1984b. "Ancient Interpretations of ὀνομαϲτὶ κωμῳδεῖν in Aristophanes." *CQ* NS 34:83-88.

Henderson, Jeffrey 1975. *The Maculate Muse: Obscene Language in Attic Comedy.* Yale University Press. New Haven.

─────── 1987. *Aristophanes: Lysistrata.* Clarendon Press. Oxford.

─────── forthcoming. "The Demos and the Comic Festival."

Herington, C. J. 1963. "Athena in Athenian Literature and Cult." *G&R* 10, Suppl.:61-73.

Hignett, C. 1952. *A History of the Athenian Constitution to the End of the Fifth Century B.C.* Clarendon Press. Oxford.

Jameson, Michael 1960. "A Decree of Themistocles from Troizen." *Hesperia* 29: 198-223.

Jocelyn, H. D. 1980. "A Greek Indecency and Its Students: ΛΑΙΚΑΖΕΙΝ," *PCPS* NS 26:12-66.

Kagan, Donald 1974. *The Archidamian War*. Ithaca and London.

Kassel, R. 1973. "Kritische und exegetische Kleinigkeiten IV." *RM* 116:97-112.

Kleinknecht, H. 1939. "Die Epiphanie des Demos in Aristophanes' 'Ritter'." *Hermes* 77: 58-65 = *Aristophanes und die alte Komödie*, ed. H. J. Newiger (Wege der Forschung 265, Wissenschaftliche Buchgesellschaft, Darmstadt, 1975), pp. 144-54 (with a one-page Korrekturnachtrag).

Kleve, K. 1964. "ΑΠΡΑΓΜΟΣΥΝΗ and ΠΟΛΥΠΡΑΓΜΟΣΥΝΗ: Two Slogans in Athenian Politics." *SO* 39:83-88.

Körte, A. 1921. "Komödie." In *RE* 11 (half vol. 21), cols. 1207-75.

Komornicka, A. M. 1964. *Métaphores, Personnifications et Comparaisons dans l'oeuvre d'Aristophane*. Komitet Nauk Kulturze Antycznej Polskiej Akademi Nauk, Archiwum Filologiczne 10. Wraclaw, Warsaw, and Cracow.

Konstan, D. and M. Dillon 1981. "The Ideology of Aristophanes' *Wealth*." *AJP* 102:371-94.

Kraus, Walther 1985. *Aristophanes' politische Komödien (Die Acharner/Die Ritter)*. Osterreichische Akademie der Wissenschaften, Philologisch-historische Klasse, Sitzungsberichte 453. Vienna.

Landfester, M. 1967. *Die Ritter des Aristophanes*. B. R. Grüner. Amsterdam.

Lanza, Diego 1977. *Il tiranno e suo pubblico*. Einaudi. Turin.

Lanza, Diego and Mario Vegetti 1977. *L'ideologia della città*. Liguori. Naples.

Lateiner, Donald 1982. "'The Man Who Does Not Meddle in Politics': A *Topos* in Lysias." *CW* 76:1-12.

Lefkowitz, Mary 1975. "The Influential Fictions in the Scholia to Pindar's *Pythian* 8." *CP* 70:179-83.

──────── 1977. "Pindar's Pythian 8." *CJ* 72:209-21.

Lévêque P. and P. Vidal-Naquet 1964. *Clisthène l'Athénien*. Les Belles Lettres. Paris.

Lévy, Edmond 1976. *Athènes devant la défaite de 404: Histoire d'une crise idéologique. Bibliothèque des Ecoles d'Athènes et de Rome*, fasc. 125. Editions de Boccard. Paris.

Lind, H. 1985. "Neues aus Kydathen: Beobachtungen zum Hintergrund der 'Daitales' und der 'Ritter' des Aristophanes." *MH* 42:249-61.

Lloyd, G. E. R. 1983. *Science, Folklore and Ideology: Studies in the Life Sciences in Ancient Greece.* Cambridge University Press. Cambridge.

Lloyd-Jones, H. 1975. "More About Antileon Tyrant of Chalcis (Solon frag. 33 and Aristophanes *Eq.* 1042-44)." *CP* 70:197.

Loraux, Nicole 1973. "'Marathon' ou l'histoire idéologique." *REA* 75:13-42.

_____ 1981. *L'invention d'Athènes: Histoire de l'oraison funèbre dans la "cité classique".* Ecole des Hautes Etudes en Sciences Sociales, Centre de Recherches Historiques, Civilisations et Sociétés 65. Mouton. Paris.

_____ 1984. "Solon au milieu de la lice." In *Aux origines de l'Hellénisme, la Crète et la Grèce: Hommage à Henri van Effenterre*, pp. 199-214. *Publications de la Sorbonne, Histoire Ancienne et Médiévale* 15. Paris.

_____ 1986. "Repolitiser la cité." *L'Homme* 26:239-55.

MacDowell, D.M. 1971. *Aristophanes: Wasps.* Clarendon Press. Oxford.

_____ 1982. "Aristophanes and Kallistratos." *CQ* 32:21-26.

Marx, Karl and Friedrich Engels 1959. *The German Ideology.* In *Karl Marx and Friedrich Engels: Basic Writings on Politics and Philosophy*, ed. Lewis S. Feuer. Anchor Books. New York.

Masaracchia, A. 1958. *Solone.* La Nuova Italia. Florence.

Mastromarco, G. 1979. "L'esordio 'segreto' di Aristofane." *Quaderni di Storia* 10:152-96.

Maxwell-Stewart, P.G. 1972. "Two Notes on Aristophanes." *Ziva Antica* 26:43-44.

Megas, G. A. 1970. *Folktales of Greece.* The University of Chicago Press. Chicago and London.

Meiggs, Russell 1972. *The Athenian Empire.* Clarendon Press. Oxford.

Mikalson, Jon D. 1975. *The Sacred and Civil Calendar of the Athenian Year.* Princeton University Press. Princeton.

_____ 1983. *Athenian Popular Religion.* University of North Carolina Press. Chapel Hill and London.

Montanari, Enrico 1981. *Il mito dell'autoctonia*, 2nd ed. Bulzoni. Rome.

Moulakis, A. 1973. *Homonoia: Eintracht und die Entwicklung eines politischen Bewusstseins*. List. Munich.

Nagy, Gregory 1979. *The Best of the Achaeans*. The Johns Hopkins University Press. Baltimore and London.

_____ 1985. "A Poet's Vision of His City." In *Theognis of Megara*, edd. T. Figueira and G. Nagy, pp. 22-76. The Johns Hopkins University Press. Baltimore and London.

_____ 1986. "Ancient Greek Epic and Praise Poetry: Some Typological Considerations." In *The Oral Tradition in Literature: Interpretation in Context*, ed. J. M. Foley, pp. 89-102.

Navarre, O. 1956. *Les Cavaliers d'Aristophane*. Editions Mellottée. Paris.

Neil, R. A. 1901. *The Knights of Aristophanes*. Cambridge University Press. Cambridge.

Nestle, W. 1927. "ΑΠΡΑΓΜΟΣΥΝΗ (Zu Thukydides II.63)." *Philologus* 81 = NF 35:129-40 = *Griechische Studien* (1948), pp. 374-86.

_____ 1938. "Der Friedengedanke in der antiken Welt." *Philologus* Suppl. vol. 31, Part 1.

Newiger, Hans-Joachim 1957. *Metapher und Allegorie*. Zetemata 16. C. H. Beck. Munich.

Nilsson, M. P. 1955. *Geschichte der griechischen Religion*, vol. 1, 2nd ed. C. H. Beck. Munich.

North, H. 1966. *Sophrosyne: Self-Knowledge and Self-Restraint in Greek Literature*. Cornell University Press. Ithaca.

Nussbaum, M. 1986. *The Fragility of Goodness*. Cambridge University Press. Cambridge.

Perusino, Franca. 1981. "Aristofane e il *Maricante* di Eupoli: Un Caso di *Contaminatio* nella Commedia Attica del V Secolo." *RFIC* 109:407-13.

_____ 1982. "Cratino, la *kline* e la lira: Una metafora ambivalente nei *Cavalieri* di Aristofane." *Corolla Londinensis* 2:147-59.

Phillips, III C. R. 1984. Rev. of de Ste. Croix 1981. *Helios* NS 1:59-60.

Pickard-Cambridge, A. W. 1962. *Dithyramb, Tragedy and Comedy*, 2nd ed. Rev. T. B. L. Webster. Clarendon Press. Oxford.

Podlecki, A. J. 1975-6. "A Pericles 'Prosopon' in Attic Tragedy?" *Evphrosyne: Revista di Filologia Classica*. NS 7:25-26.

Pohlenz, M. 1952. "Aristophanes' Ritter." *Nachrichten der Akademie der Wissenschaften in Göttingen*, philologisch-historische Klasse 5 = *Kleine Schriften* (1965), vol. 2, pp. 519ff.

Prato, C. 1962. *I canti di Aristofane*. Ateneo. Rome.

Radt, S. L. 1958. *Pindars Zweiter und Sechster Paian*. Hakkert. Amsterdam.

Rau, P. 1967. *Paratragodia*. Munich.

Renehan, R. 1969. *Greek Textual Criticism: A Reader*. Cambridge, MA.

_____ 1976. *Studies in Greek Texts*. Hypomnemata 43. Göttingen.

Richards, I. A. 1965. *The Philosophy of Rhetoric*. Oxford University Press. New York.

Romilly, J. de 1972. "Le mot ὁμόνοια: Vocabulaire et propagande." In *Etudes et Commentaires 79, Melanges de linguistique et de philologie grecques offerts à Pierre Chantraine*, pp. 199-209. Klincksieck. Lille.

Rose, H. J. 1960. *A Handbook of Greek Literature*. Dutton. New York.

Rosen, Ralph M. 1983. "Old Comedy and the Iambographic Tradition." Ph.D. diss. Harvard University.

Rusten, Jeffrey 1983. "ΓΕΙΤΩΝ ΗΡΩΣ: Pindar's Prayer to Heracles (*N.* 7.86-101) and Greek Popular Religion." *HSCP* 87:289-97.

Sandys, J. E. 1893. *Aristotle's Constitution of Athens*. London.

Schein, Seth 1985. "ΣΥΝ ᾿ΑΡΤΕΜΕΕΣΣΙ ΦΙΛΟΙΣΙΝ: *ODYSSEY* 13.43." *SIFC* 3:27-28.

Schwinge, E.-R. 1975a. "Kritik und Komik: Gedanken zu Aristophanes' Wespen," in *Dialogos: Für Harald Patzer zum 65. Geburtstag*, edd. Justus Cobet, R. Leimbach, and A. B. Neschke-Hentschke, pp. 35-47. Wiesbaden.

_____ 1975b. "Zur Ästhetik der aristophanischen Komödie am Beispiel der Ritter." *Maia* 27:177-99.

Segal, Charles 1976. "Pindar, Mimnermus, and the 'Zeus-given Gleam': the End of Pythian 8." *QUCC* 22:71-81.

Siewert, P. 1979. "Poseidon Hippios am Kolonos und die athenischen Hippeis." In

Arktouros (B. M. W. Knox Festschrift), edd. G. W. Bowersock et al., pp. 280-289. Walter de Gruyter. Berlin and New York.

Sifakis, G. M. 1971. *Parabasis and Animal Chorus.* London.

Silk, Michael 1974. *Interaction in Poetic Imagery.* Cambridge University Press. Cambridge.

Slater, W.J. 1976. "Symposium at Sea." *HSCP* 80:161-70.

_____ 1979. "Pindar's Myths: Two Pragmatic Explanations." In *Arktouros* (B. M. W. Knox Festschrift), edd. G. W. Bowersock et al., pp. 69-70. Walter de Gruyter. Berlin and New York.

Sommerstein, A. H. 1977. "Aristophanes and the events of 411." *JHS* 97:112-26.

_____ 1980a. "Notes on Aristophanes' Knights." *CQ* NS 30:46-56.

_____ 1980b. *Acharnians. The Comedies of Aristophanes*, vol. 1. Aris and Phillips, Ltd. Warminster.

_____ 1981. *Knights. The Comedies of Aristophanes*, vol. 2. Aris and Phillips, Ltd. Warminster.

_____ 1982. *Clouds. The Comedies of Aristophanes*, vol. 3. Aris and Phillips, Ltd. Warminster.

_____ 1983. *Wasps. The Comedies of Aristophanes*, vol. 4. Aris and Phillips, Ltd. Warminster.

_____ 1986. "The Decree of Syrakosios." *CQ* 36:101-108

Spyropoulos, E. 1981. "ὄνεια πράγματα." *Hellenica* 33:3-13.

Ste. Croix, G. E. M. de 1972. *The Origins of the Peloponnesian War.* Duckworth. London.

_____ 1981. *The Class Struggle in the Ancient Greek World from the Archaic Age to the Arab Conquests.* Duckworth. London.

Stinton, T. C. W. 1976. "Solon, Fragment 25." *JHS* 96:160

Strauss, Leo 1966. *Socrates and Aristophanes.* Basic Books. New York and London.

Taillardat, J. 1965. *Les images d'Aristophane: Etudes de langue et de style*, 2nd ed. Les Belles Lettres. Paris.

Taplin, O. 1983. "Tragedy and Trugedy." *CQ* 33:331-34.

Taylor, Michael 1981. *The Tyrant Slayers: The Heroic Image in Fifth Century BC Athenian Art and Politics. Monographs in Classical Studies.* Arno Press. New York.

Tod, M. N. 1933. *A Selection of Greek Historical Inscriptions.* 2 vols. Oxford.

Turato, Fabio 1979. *La crisi della città e l'ideologia del selvaggio nell'Atene del V secolo a.C.* Edizioni dell'Ateneo e Bizzarri. Rome.

Van Nes, D. 1963. *Die Maritime Bildersprache des Aischylos.* J. B. Wolters. Groningen.

Vernant, J.-P. 1969. *Les origines de la pensée grecque.* Presses Universitaires de Paris. Paris.

_____ 1971. *Mythe et pensée chez les Grecs,* vol. 1. Maspero. Paris.

Vlastos, Gregory 1946. "Solonian Justice." *CP* 41:65-83.

_____ 1947. "Equality and Justice in Early Greek Cosmologies." *CP* 42:156-78.

Wade-Gery, H. T. 1932. "Thucydides the Son of Melesias." *JHS* 52:205-227.

Welsh, D. 1978. "The Development of the Relation Between Aristophanes and Cleon to 424 B.C." Ph.D. diss. King's College, University of London.

_____ 1979. "*Knights* 230-3 and Cleon's Eyebrows." *CQ* NS 29:214-15.

West, D. J. 1977. *Homosexuality Re-examined.* London.

West, M. L. 1966. *Hesiod: Theogony.* Clarendon Press. Oxford.

_____ 1974. *Studies in Greek Elegy and Iambus.* Walter de Gruyter. New York and Berlin.

Wilamowitz, U. von 1893. *Aristoteles und Athen,* vol. 2. Weidmann. Berlin.

_____ 1921. *Griechische Verskunst.* Weidmann. Berlin.

_____ 1922. *Pindaros.* Weidmann. Berlin.

Zeitlin, F. 1982. "Travesties of Gender and Genre in Aristophanes' Thesmophoriazusae." In *Reflections of Women in Antiquity,* ed. H. Foley, pp. 169-217. Gordon and Breach. London.

Zimmermann, Bernhard 1984, 1985, 1987. *Untersuchungen zur Form und dramatischen Technik der Aristophanischen Komödien.* Vol. 1: Parodos und Amoibaion. Vol. 2: Die anderen lyrischen Partien. Beiträge zur klassischen Philologie 154,

166. Verlag Anton Hain. Königstein/Ts. Vol. 3: Metrische Analysen. Beiträge zur klassischen Philologie 178. Athenäum Verlag. Frankfurt am Main.

Ziolkowski, J. E. 1981. *Thucydides and the Tradition of Funeral Speeches at Athens.* Monographs in Classical Studies. Arno Press. New York.

702-704: 40
702: 51n4
709: 51n4
730-33: 71 (Appendix)
736-40: 48, 72 (Appendix)
738: 48
742-43: 51n4
751: 74 (Appendix)
756-57: 6n7, 7
761-2: 7
763-64: 40n12, 41, 46
763-823: 72 (Appendix), 73 (Appendix)
766: 51n4
771: 51
786-87: 15n43
786: 15n44, 72 (Appendix)
794: 69 (Appendix), 794: 72 (Appendix)
797: 72 (Appendix)
801-802: 54n16
811-12: 41, 46
811-19: 69 (Appendix), 72 (Appendix)
813: 72 (Appendix)
814-16: 46n21
814: 72 (Appendix)
817-18: 52
823: 52
830: 7
831: 52
839-40: 7n9
840: 1n2
843-46: 51n4
843-910: 72 (Appendix), 73 (Appendix)
847: 73 (Appendix)
852-54: 15, 15n43
863: 52n7
864-67: 7
867: 1n2
877-80: 73 (Appendix)
902: 1n2, 6
930-33: 54n16
947-59: 36
954: 52
984: 2
1017-24: 55

1018: 52n7
1023: 52n7
1030: 56
1036-44: 73 (Appendix), 74 (Appendix)
1037: 36n4, 7: 73 (Appendix)
1042-44: 15n43, 73 (Appendix)
1044: 15n43
1052-61: 51n4
1060: 67 (Appendix)
1065-66: 47
1090-91: 40n12
1103: 73 (Appendix)
1111-50: 73 (Appendix)
1150: 74 (Appendix)
1166-67: 51n4
1169-76: 40n13
1171-72: 40n12
1172: 67 (Appendix)
1177: 40n12
1181-82: 40n12
1225: 74 (Appendix)
1236: 52n6
1242: 74 (Appendix)
1245-47: 74 (Appendix)
1249: 74 (Appendix)
1250-52: 74 (Appendix)
1256: 73 (Appendix)
1264-1315: 74 (Appendix)
1274-89: 49
1288-89: 49n31
1300-04: 74 (Appendix)
1321: 43, 47, 48
1323: 43
1325: 46, 47
1326-27: 43
1326-34: 43n3, 74 (Appendix)
1327: 43
1329: 43
1330: 47, 73 (Appendix), 74 (Appendix)
1331: 44
1332: 44 and 44n5
1333: 47, 48
1334: 44, 44n8, 46
1349: 43, 43n2
1350-53: 47
1350-55: 46, 46n21

Hippias frag. 26.1-3 W: 7n11

Homer

   Il.
      1.579: 7
      2.95 : 7
      7.345-46: 7
      8.86: 5
      9 (without line reference): 22
      13.798: 9
      16.282: 22
      18.508: 36n8
      23.204: 11n29
   Od.
      1.411: 29
      2.16: 43n2
      3.19-20: 43n2
      4.64: 29
      4.204-205: 43n2
      5.285: 6
      5.291-97: 7n9
      5.304: 6
      14.300: 11n27
      15.479: 23n13
      24.252: 29
   schol. *Il.* 8.368: 56n24

Inscriptions

   ATL 1.155, ll.57-8: 45n15
   IG I^{2}120: 20n18
   IG I^{2}946: 39
   IG ii^{2}5222: 40n7
   IG ii^{2}5765: 15n44
   IG II^{2}2343: 61n13

Isocrates

   7.48: 43
   18.44: 20n18
   Antid. 151: 20n17

Pausanias

   2.29.2: 28n42
   8.11.3: 49
   10.9.11: 9

Phocus fr. 33a W: 8

Pindar

   Isth.
      2.8: 21
      5.22: 25
      7.38: 31n4
      9.3: 24
   Nem.
      1.21-22: 27
      3.3: 24
      4.95-96: 23
      9.48: 21
   Ol.
      2.63: 6
      2.90: 21
      4.20: 24
      7.30: 5
      8.30: 24
      13 (without line reference): 24n19
   Pyth.
      1.92: 36n6
      1.98: 21
      5.10: 31n4
      5.99-100: 21
      8.1-2: 23, 25
      8.2-3: 25
      8.3-4: 23
      8.6-7: 21, 23
      8.8-14: 24
      8.9-10: 23n12, 31n3
      8.10: 23
      8.12: 23, 35n2
      8.14: 23
      8.16: 24
      8.17-18: 23n15
      8.17: 23
      8.19-20: 24
      8.20: 22n7
      8.22-24: 24
      8.22-24: 28
      8.22: 23, 27
      8.24-25: 28
      8.31-32: 22
      8.31: 21
      8.35-37: 29

41: 36
42: 36, 36n6
43: 35
46: 36, 36n6
48: 36
51: 35
52: 36n5
219: 8
219-20: 12-13
290: 36n6
495: 13
543-46: 13
667-82: 12
675-78: 12
678: 11n30, 13, 36n7
679: 15
680: 6n7
681: 25
854: 56n23
945-46: 13
1081-82: 35
1222:5
1312: 27n33

Theopompus *FGrH* 115F93: 5

Thrasymachus B1 (D-K II.323.4 and 324.1): 8n13

Thucydides

    1.6.3: 43, 45
    1.6.3: 46n19
    1.70.8: 19
    1.70.8-9: 29, 31
    1.95.1: 45
    1.96: 45
    1.141.6: 45
    2.35-46: 44
    2.38.1: 45
    2.39.1: 45
    2.39.2-4-46: 45
    2.40.1: 45
    2.40.2: 18
    2.41.1: 45
    2.63.2: 18
    2.63: 47n23
    2.65.7: 32

2.65: 36n9
2.70.4: 69 (Appendix)
2.84.2-3: 8, 32n3
3.11.7: 54n16
3.36.6: 32, 48
3.37: 47n23
3.42.2: 32
3.79.3: 8n13
3.82-83: 2, 14n34
3.82.2: 14n33, 32
3.82.8: 32
4.27.5: 6, 19
4.28.5: 19n13
4.40.2: 19n12
4.42-44: 41
4.44.1: 41
4.75.1 : 8n13
4.96.3: 8
4.118.11: 55n19
5.7.3: 51n3
5.16.1: 32, 55n19
5.25.1: 8n12
5.43.2: 55n19
6.18.7: 20
6.56.2: 15
6.57.1: 15
6.87.3: 19
7.44: 8
7.57.4: 45n13
7.80.3: 8
7.81.2: 8
7.84.4: 8
7.86.4 : 8n13
8.47-48.1: 64
8.71.1: 32n3
8.73: 64n24
8.75.2 : 20n18
8.79.1: 8n13
8.93.3: 20n18

Timocreon

    PMG 727: 46n21
    PMG 731: 71 (Appendix)

Xenophon

    Anab.

1.8.2: 8n12
3.1.21: 11n29
de re eq. or *Eq.*
   1.3: 61
   9.4: 5
   11.6: 61
Hell. 5.2.35: 8n12
Mem.
   2.9.1: 14
   4.4.8: 14
Oec.
   8.4: 8n12, 24n18
   8.7: 24
Sym. 6.6: 61
Vect. 5.8 : 8n12

Xenophanes frag. 1.21-32 W: 23n14